LIGHT IN THE SHADOWS

LIGHT IN THE SHADOWS

Barbara Milman

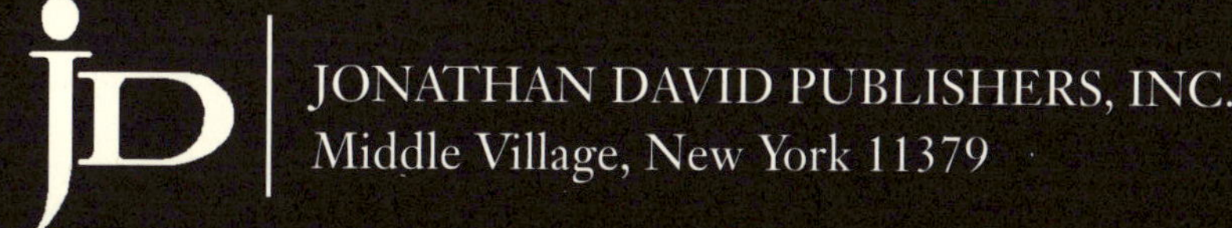
JONATHAN DAVID PUBLISHERS, INC.
Middle Village, New York 11379

LIGHT IN THE SHADOWS

Address all inquiries to:

Jonathan David Publishers, Inc.
68-22 Eliot Ave.
Middle Village, NY 11379

2 4 6 8 10 9 7 5 3 1

Library of Congress Cataloging-in-Publication Data

Milman, Barbara,
Light in the shadows / by Barbara Milman
p. cm.
ISBN 0-8246-0401-6
1. Milman, Barbara — Themes, motives. 2. Holocaust, Jewish (1939-1945), in art. 3. Holocaust, Jewish (1939–1945). I. Title.
NE1336.M55A4 1997
940.53'18—dc21

97-14067
CIP
r97

Designed and composed by John Reinhardt Book Design

Printed in the United States of America

ACKNOWLEDGMENTS

MY PROFOUND THANKS to the five people of courage who made this book possible: Peter Schrag ("Escape"); Rita Kuhn ("Berlin"); Hielke Sheneman ("Holland"); Alexander Groth ("Warsaw"), and Gloria Lyon ("Auschwitz"). Their willingness to share very painful memories of the Holocaust with me—a total stranger to all but one—was remarkable.

Many people were a source of great encouragement to me; and I regret that I cannot thank them all individually. However, I must mention the San Francisco Holocaust Oral History Project, which put me in touch with my first subjects; my friend and fellow-artist Brookes Byrd, whose critical eye and etching press both assisted me greatly in the early stages of this project; Rabbi Alfred J. Kolatch, whose belief in this book is responsible for its publication; and, finally, my husband, Daniel Rancour-Laferriere, who provided loving support and persistent enthusiasm throughout this project.

CONTENTS

PREFACE

Of the approximately nine million Jews who lived in Europe between 1933 and 1945, only one-third survived the Nazi genocide. Many Jews who managed to escape Hitler's Final Solution, and many of the non-Jews who helped save them, are still alive to describe their experiences. This book pays tribute—through word and image—to five of those people of immense courage.

In 1994 I decided to interview Holocaust survivors and create a series of prints based on their stories. I then approached the San Francisco Holocaust Oral History Project, which graciously put me in touch with several survivors. Two of these individuals, Rita Kuhn ("Berlin") and Gloria Lyon ("Auschwitz"), were the first of my interviewees. Subsequently, other subjects were suggested by friends and acquaintances, and I interviewed three more individuals: Peter Schrag ("Escape"), Alexander Groth ("Warsaw"), and Hielke Sheneman ("Holland").

The interviews were difficult for both me and my subjects. Even those who had told their stories in public forums many times found the detailed retelling very painful. As I listened, I was impressed by the strength and determination of these people, as well as by the way they downplayed their courage. Hielke Sheneman, a gentile who worked for the Dutch underground as a teenager commented, "When you don't have anything you're not brave, you're just trying to survive."

I was also struck by the role that chance plays in survival. Virtually every survivor's story reveals occasions of good fortune and coincidence, which the survivors were able to take advantage of by quick thinking, courage, and fortitude. As Alexander Groth remarked after relating how his grandparents had been killed in the Warsaw Ghetto, "Finally I understood it would take a miracle for us to survive."

The five stories retold here also show how important was the generosity of non-Jews, often strangers, in helping Jews to survive. Sometimes the gestures were seemingly small, such as leaving a piece of bread for a starving Jew, but sometimes they were enormous. As shown particularly in one story in this volume—that of a Dutch woman who hid three Jews in her house for three years—the help of non-Jews was sometimes offered at great risk.

When I completed a story and gave the subject a copy of the prints depicting his or her Holocaust experience, I was gratified to be told, "Yes, that is exactly how it was; it is just how it looked." But I also wondered at this reaction. After all, I had not been there; the images could not possibly be accurate representations of what had happened. I concluded that my prints had captured an emotional truth and created an aura of verisimilitude.

The experiences of the subjects of this volume are unique, but they are also in some ways typical. Like Alexander Groth, Rita Kuhn, Gloria Lyon, Peter Schrag, and Hielke Sheneman, a great many Jews and gentiles faced the Nazis with intelligence, courage, and determination. These special individuals, blessed with luck in addition to courage, survived.

Light in the Shadows will give you a glimpse of what occurred during the Holocaust. It is my hope that telling these stories today, one-half century after they happened, will make it less likely that similar stories will have to be told in the future.

Barbara Milman

HISTORICAL NOTE

HATRED OF THE JEWS was the cornerstone of Adolf Hitler's political philosophy, and he made it the centerpiece of Nazi rule in Germany from 1933 until his death at the end of World War II. Anti-Semitic laws and episodes of violence caused hundreds of thousands of Jews to flee Europe between 1933 and 1939, when the last avenues of escape were closed. Of the estimated 8.3 million Jews remaining in Europe between 1939 and 1945, more than six million were murdered by the Nazis. Millions were gassed at Auschwitz, Treblinka, Maidanek, and other death camps; millions more were systematically shot or starved to death. Many of those who survived, their families and homes destroyed, left Europe for good after the war. Although Hitler may not have succeeded in his dream of establishing a "Thousand-Year Reich [German state]" in Europe, he came close to his goal of destroying European Jewry. In the wake of the Holocaust, the once thriving Jewish population of Europe had almost completely vanished.

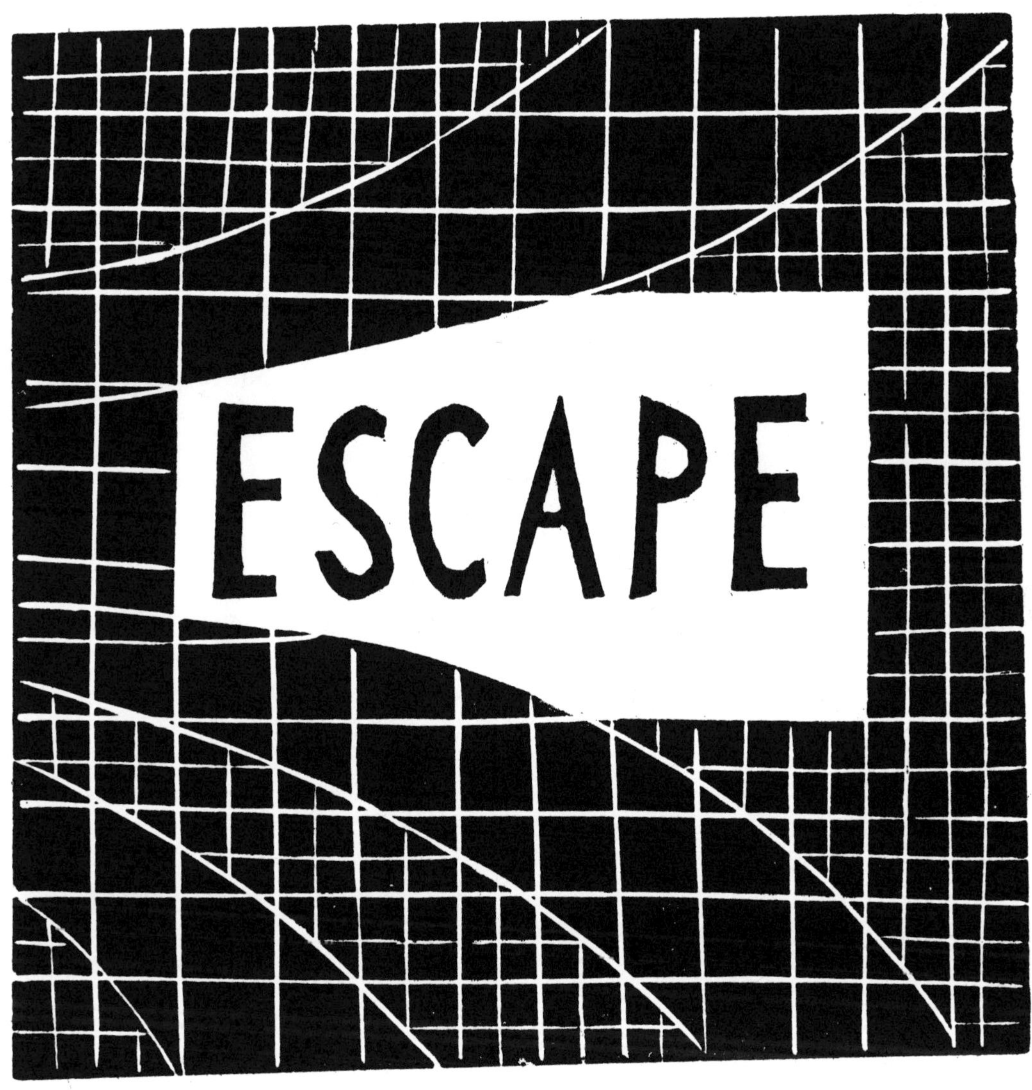
ESCAPE

Approximately 525,000 Jews lived in Germany when Hitler became that country's Chancellor in 1933. As soon as the Nazis assumed power, anti-Semitic policies were established, and Jews were increasingly barred from schools, businesses, and professions. Jewish businesses were boycotted and Jews were subjected to mistreatment and arbitrary arrest.

In 1935, the Reichstag, the national legislative body of Germany, met in the City of Nuremberg and passed the Nuremberg Laws, which stripped Jews of their German citizenship and prohibited them from marrying or having sexual relations with non-Jews. All Jews, even individuals such as **Peter Schrag**'s grandfather, who had fought in the German army in World War I, or those who held important government positions, were subject to these discriminatory laws.

With the implementation of the Nuremberg Laws, Jews with means began to leave their homeland. Peter Schrag and his family were among those Jews who fled Germany in 1935. By 1939, the year in which the war began, over 280,000 German Jews had managed to escape or emigrate to neighboring countries such as Luxembourg, which borders Germany on the west, and Belgium, which borders on Luxembourg.

By the summer of 1939, there were widespread rumors that Germany was about to start a war, and in fact World War II officially began on September 1, 1939, when Hitler's army invaded Poland to the east. Many of the Eastern European countries became allied with Germany, and in 1940 Hitler attacked Western Europe, invading Luxembourg on May 9, Belgium on May 10, and France on May 17. Ironically, German Jews like Peter Schrag's father, who had fled Nazi persecution in Germany, were treated as "enemy aliens" by the Belgians and the French. When Germany attacked, they were sent to internment camps.

It was not long before the Germans achieved victory. Belgium fell to the Nazis after only eighteen days of fighting; Paris fell on June 14; and on June 22 France and Germany signed a cease-fire agreement and the Germans took control of the northern part of the country. By the end of June 1940, the Nazis had occupied most of Western Europe and began to send refugees who had tried to escape the German advance back to their homes.

The Nazis permitted the southern part of France to remain nominally free, ruled by a collaborationist government in the city of Vichy. Jews were relatively safe in Vichy France until near the end of the war. Nevertheless, after the fall of France in 1940, tens of thousands of Jews fled from Vichy France to Spain and Portugal, both of which remained neutral throughout the war.

Peter Schrag and his family were among those Jews who escaped first to Vichy France, and then to Spain and to Portugal. From Lisbon, the Schrag family came to the United States, arriving in New York City in June 1941. By that time most countries, including the United States, were severely restricting the immigration of European Jews. Peter and his family only had a three-month transit visa to Mexico. After Pearl Harbor, they were given a visitor's visa, but they did not become permanent residents of the United States until long after the war had ended.

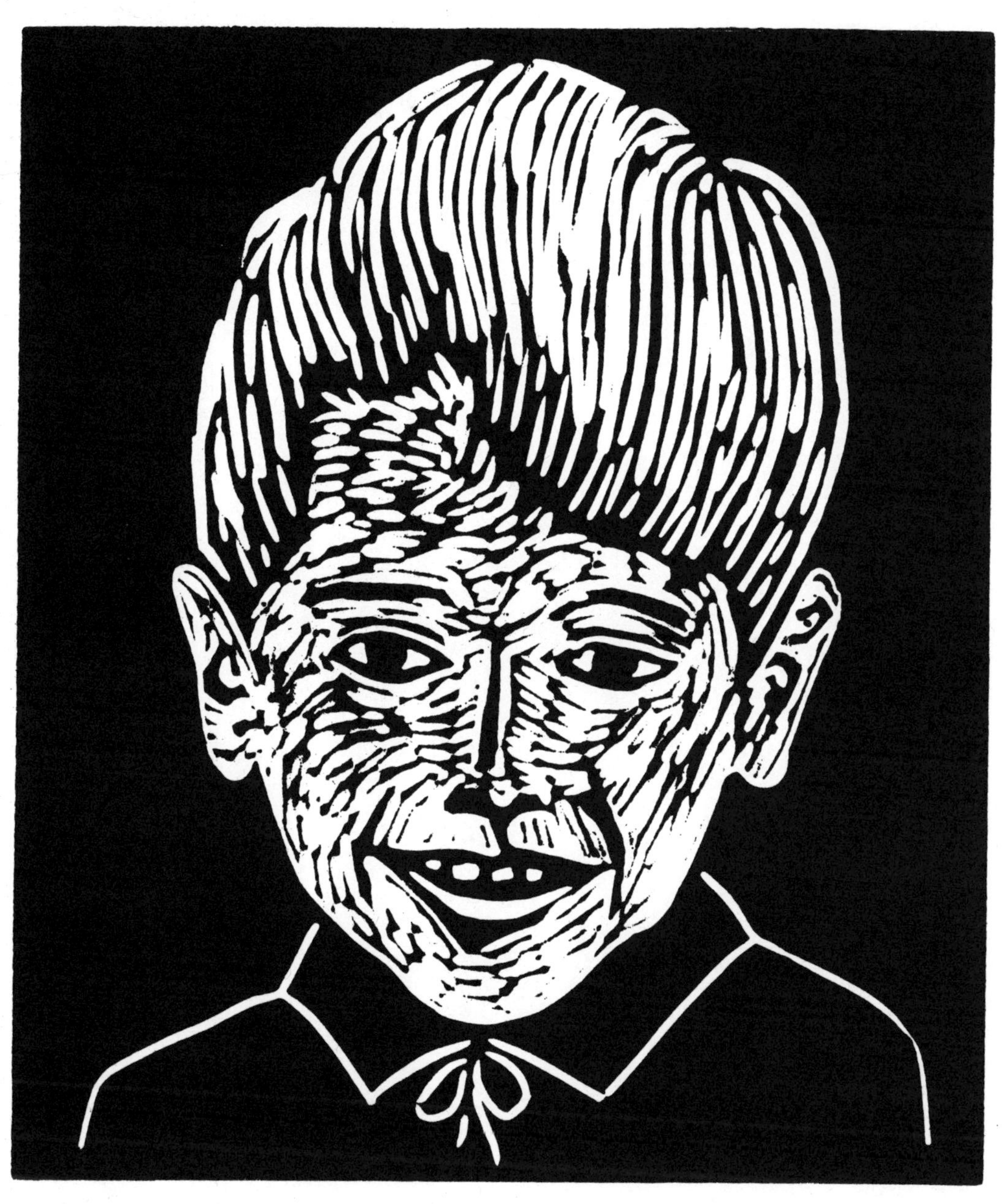

I WAS BORN IN 1931 INTO A PROSPEROUS GERMAN JEWISH FAMILY. MY GRANDFATHER WAS A SENIOR GERMAN ARMY OFFICER IN WORLD WAR I AND LATER A DEPUTY IN THE REICHSTAG. MY FATHER RAN A FAMILY BUSINESS. IN 1935, THE YEAR OF THE NUREMBERG LAWS, MY FAMILY MOVED TO LUXEMBOURG.

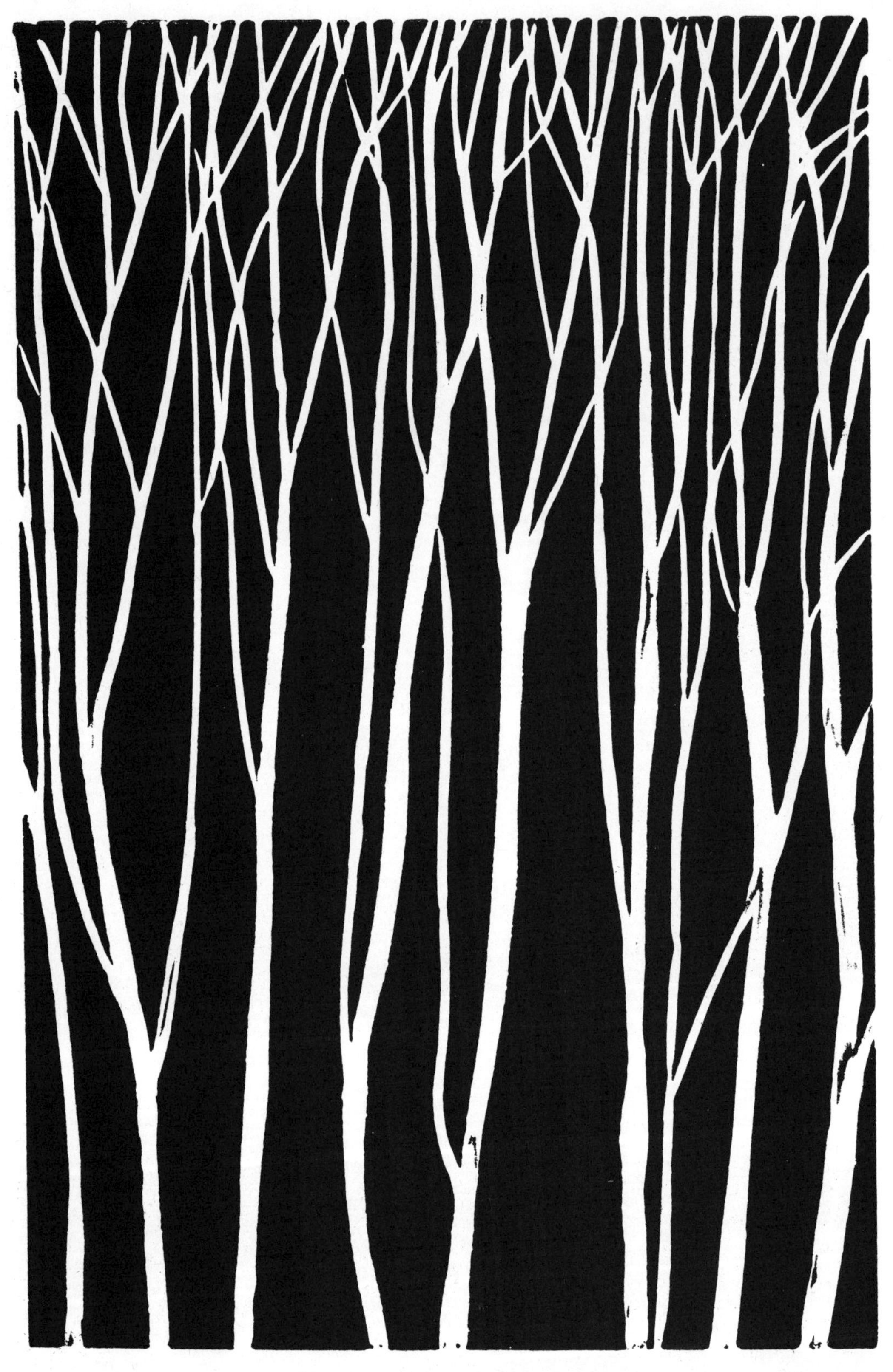

SUMMER, 1939. WALKING IN THE WOODS NEAR THE BORDER I AND MY COUSIN HEARD MEN SPEAKING GERMAN. TERRIFIED, WE FLED. SOON AFTER WE MOVED TO BRUSSELS.

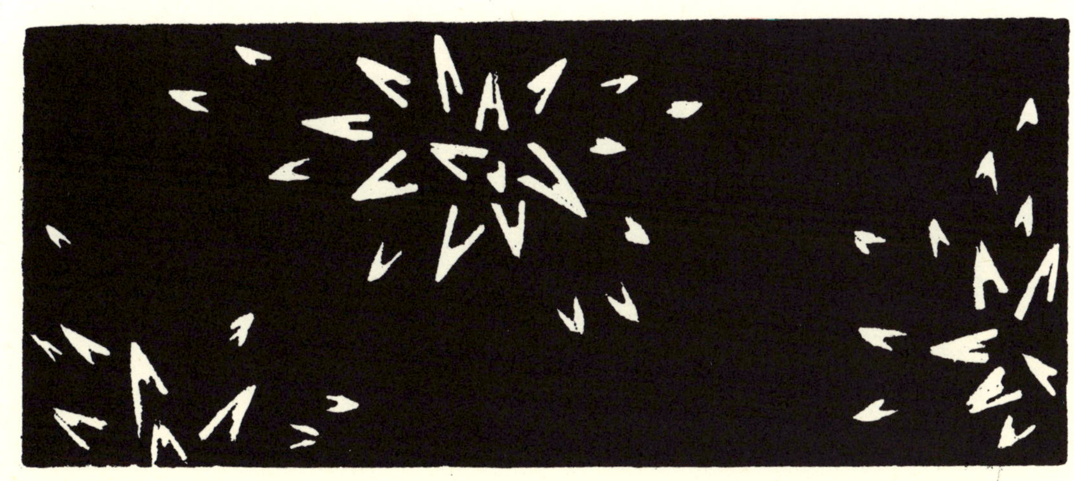

MAY 10, 1940. GERMANY ATTACKED BELGIUM. MY FATHER WAS PROMPTLY INTERNED AS AN ENEMY ALIEN AND SENT TO A CAMP IN FRANCE. WHEN AIR RAIDS BEGAN AT NIGHT WE TOOK SHELTER IN A CELLAR. ON MAY 16 MY MOTHER, MY GRANDMOTHER AND I SET OUT TOWARDS THE FRENCH COAST, HOPING TO ESCAPE FROM THE GERMAN ADVANCE INTO BELGIUM.

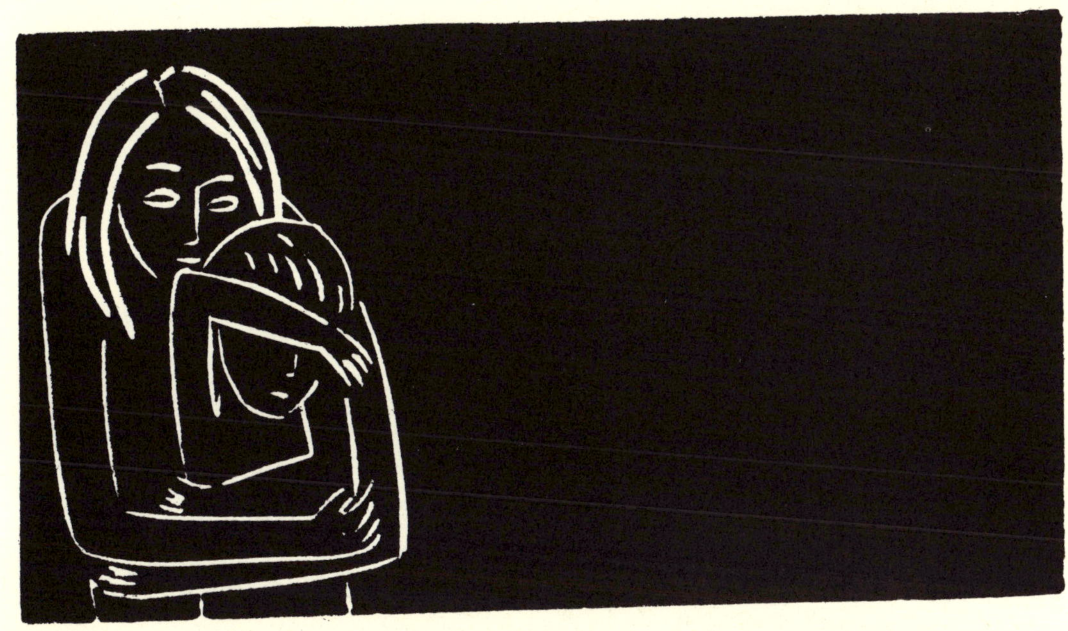

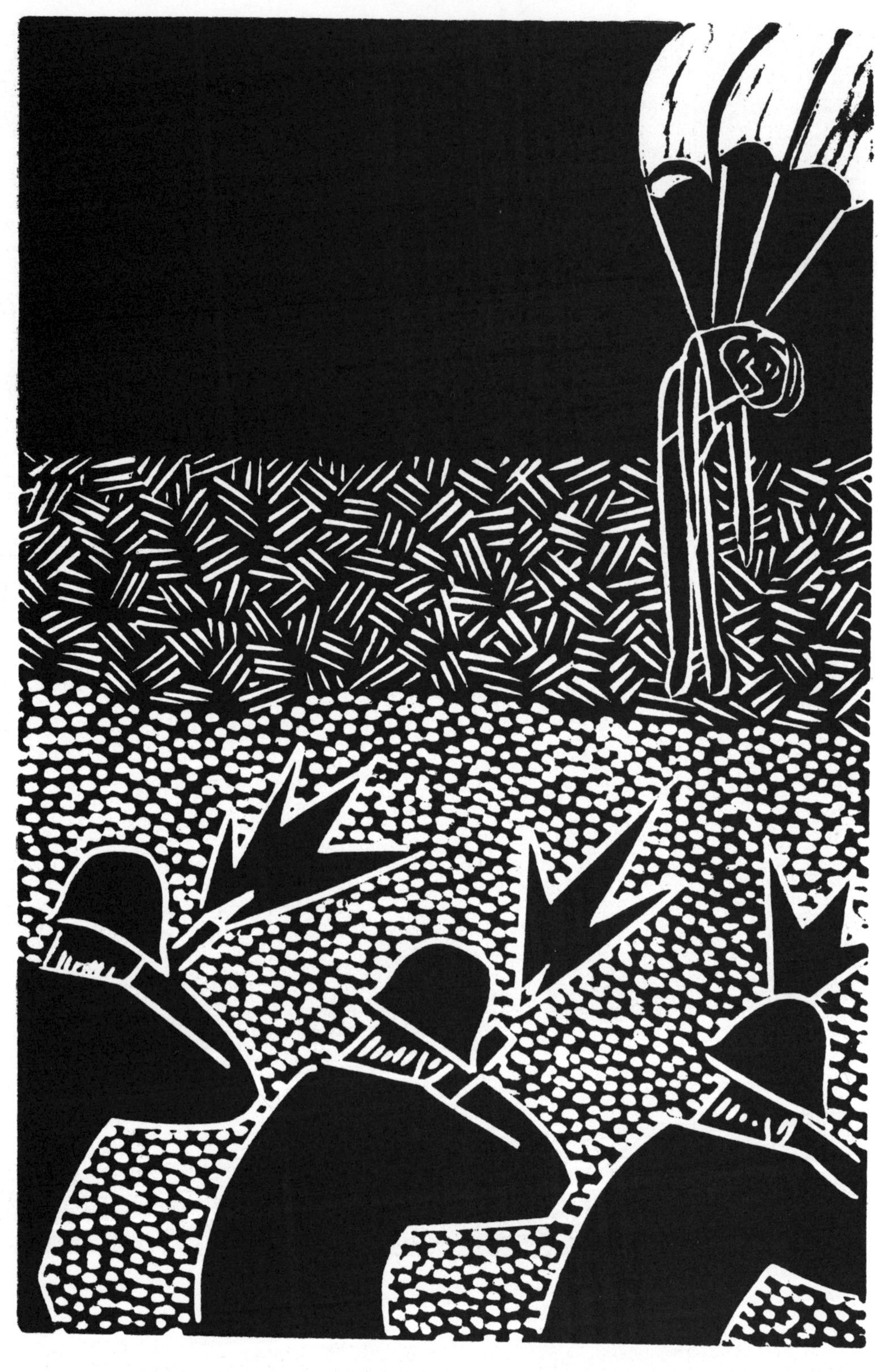

WE STOPPED IN DePANNE BECAUSE OUR CAR BROKE DOWN. GERMAN PLANES WERE CIRCLING THE BEACH. A PLANE WAS HIT AND THE PILOT PARACHUTED DOWN. THE BELGIAN GENDARMES SHOT HIM IN THE AIR.

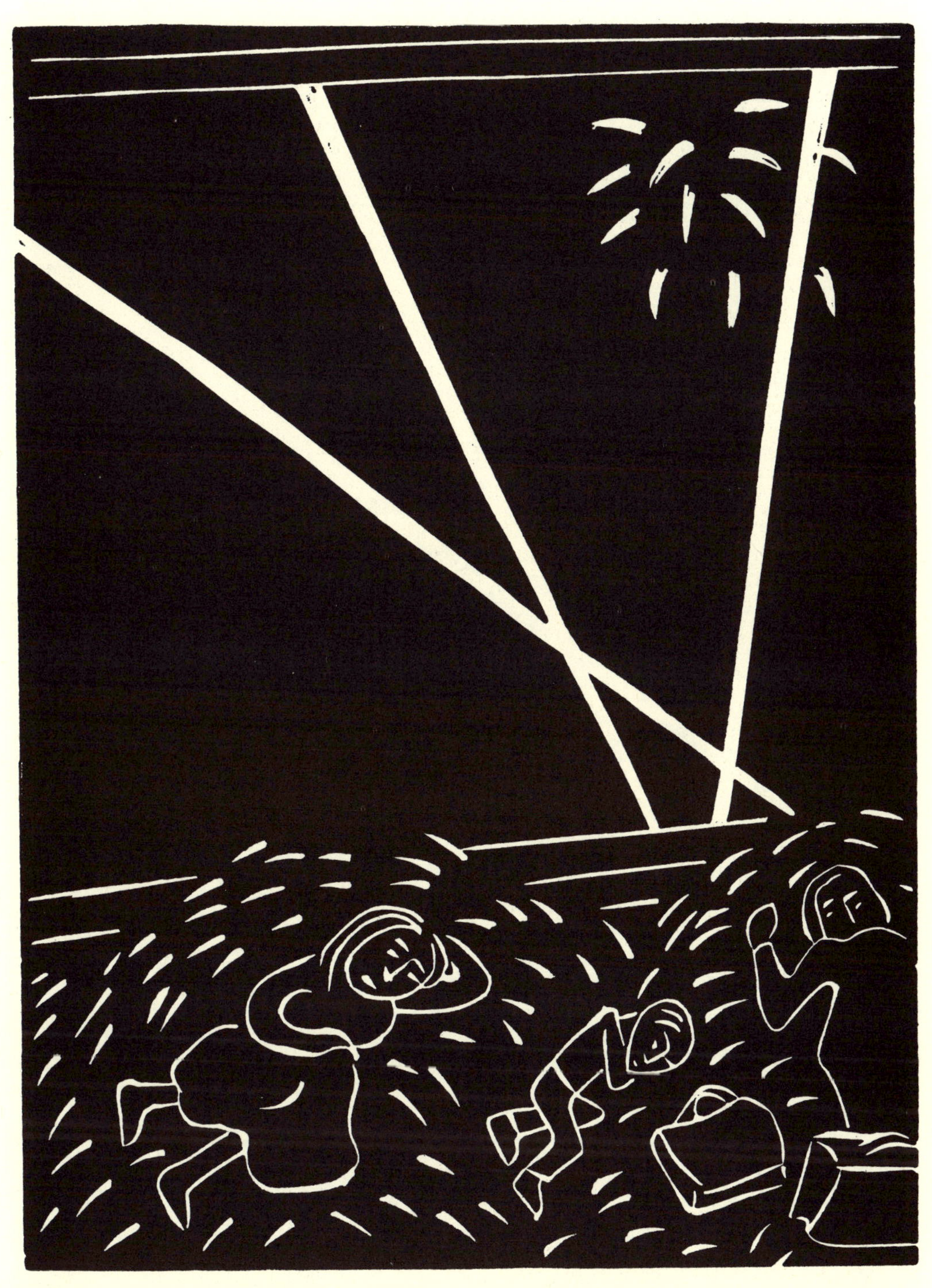

OVERNIGHT OUR DRIVER STOLE OUR CAR. WE SPENT THE NEXT NIGHT IN A HAYLOFT. WE COULD SEE SEARCHLIGHTS AND ANTI-AIRCRAFT FIRE. THE NEXT DAY WE BOUGHT ANOTHER CAR, AND A BELGIAN OFFICER DROVE US ACROSS THE FRENCH BORDER TO BOULOGNE.

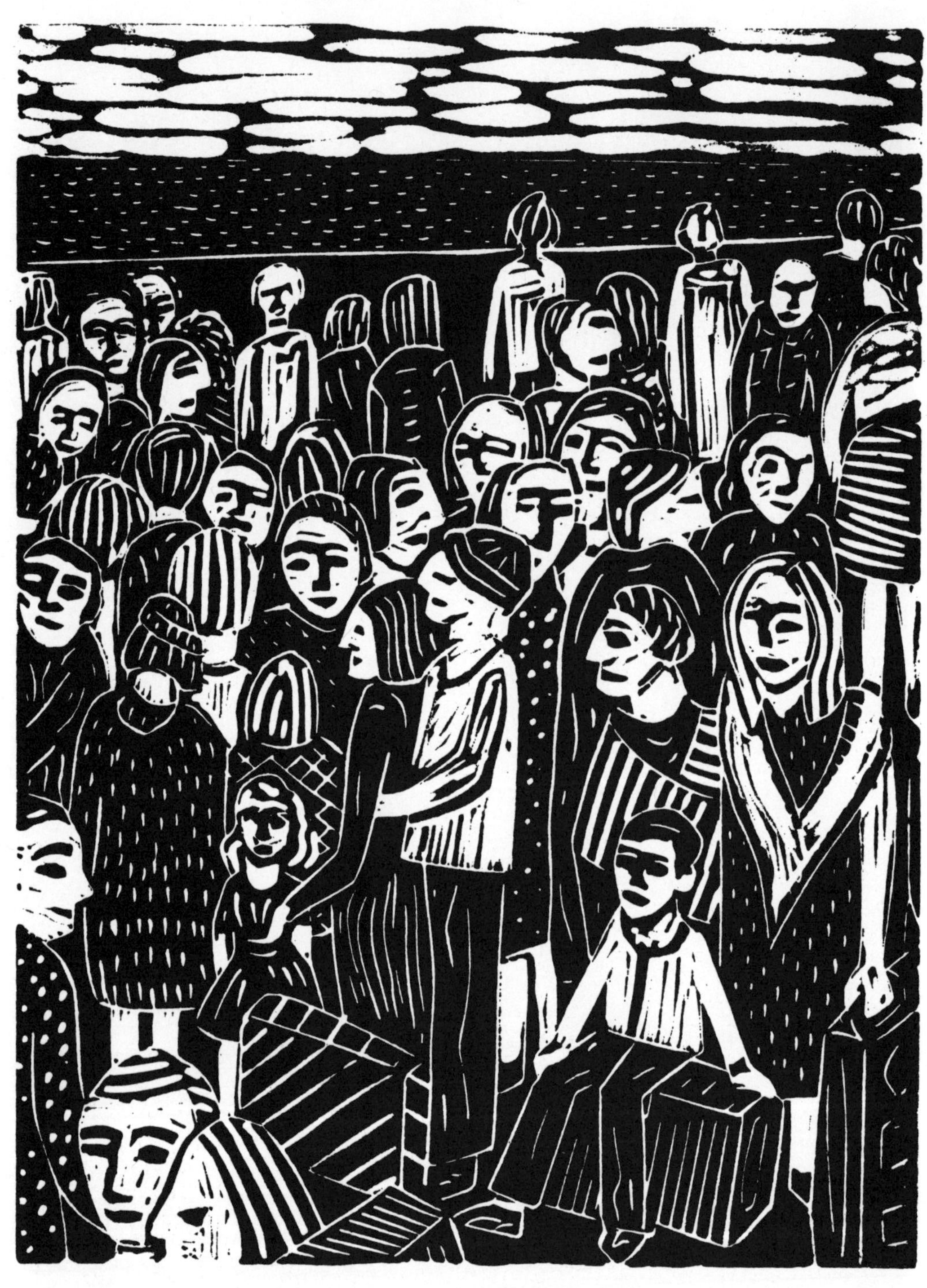

AT THE HARBOR IN BOULOGNE WE JOINED THOUSANDS OF OTHER REFUGEES. THE GERMANS WERE BOMBING THE CITY. WE SPENT THE NEXT FEW DAYS IN A DARK, CROWDED CELLAR. WHEN THERE WAS A LULL IN THE BOMBING WE WENT OUT TO LOOK FOR FOOD.

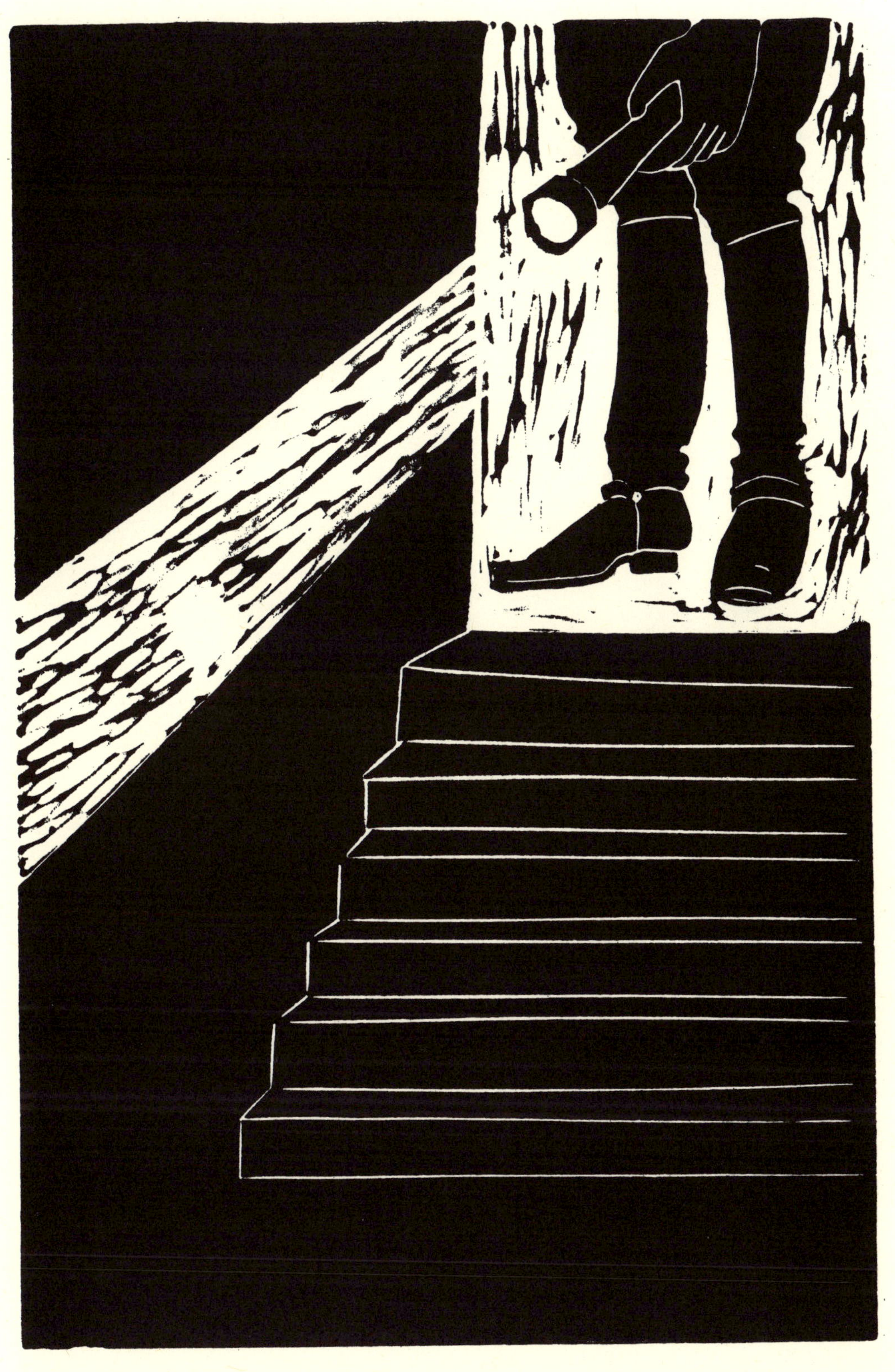

MAY 25. AFTER DAYS OF BOMBS AND GUNFIRE, THERE WAS A SUDDEN SILENCE. WE DID NOT KNOW WHO HAD WON. THEN THE CELLAR DOOR WAS OPENED BY SOLDIERS YELLING, "ALLE RAUS."

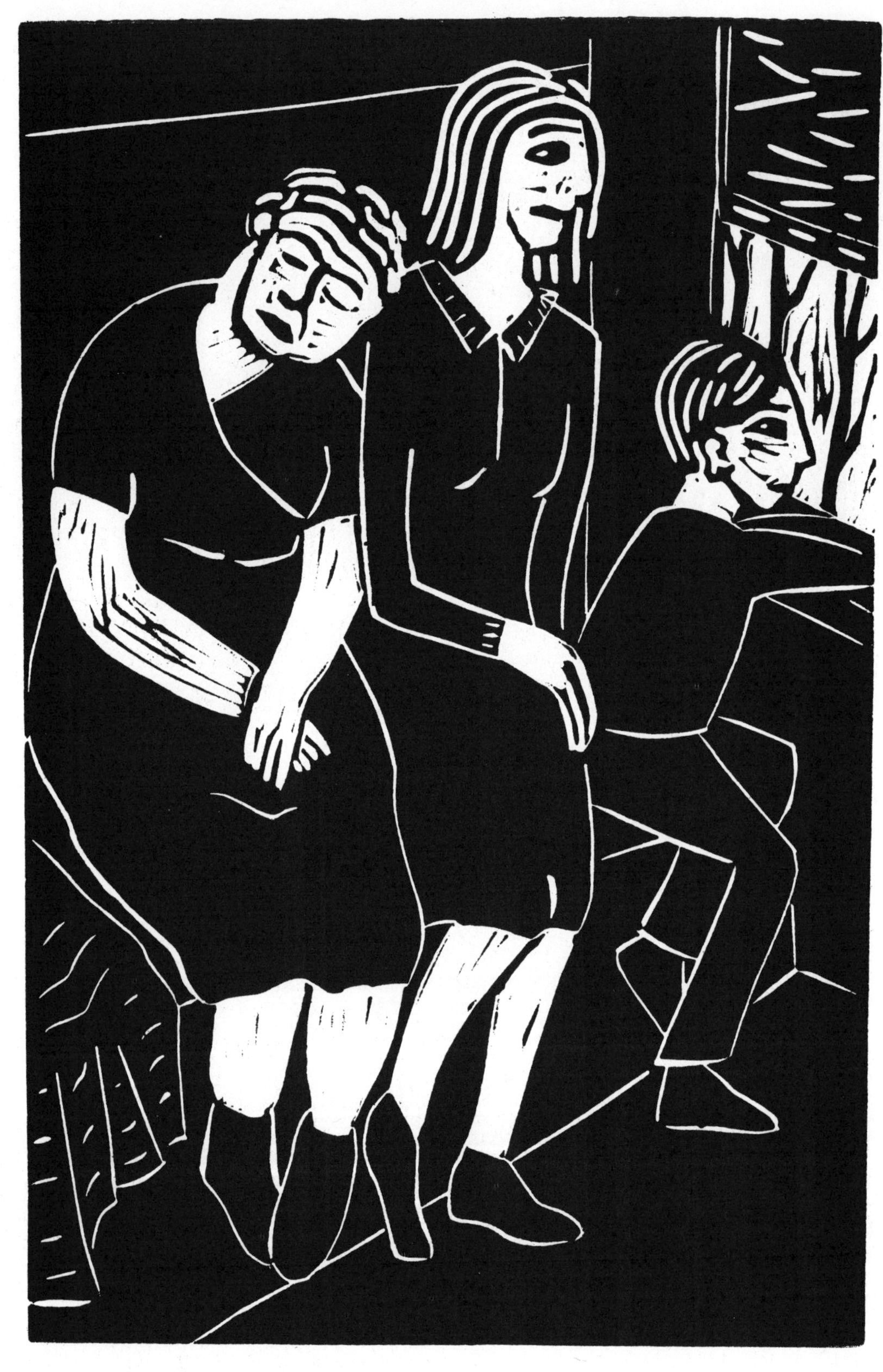

IN MID-JUNE THE GERMANS
REPATRIATED ALL REFUGEES.
WE WERE SENT BACK TO BELGIUM.
OUR ESCAPE ATTEMPT HAD FAILED.

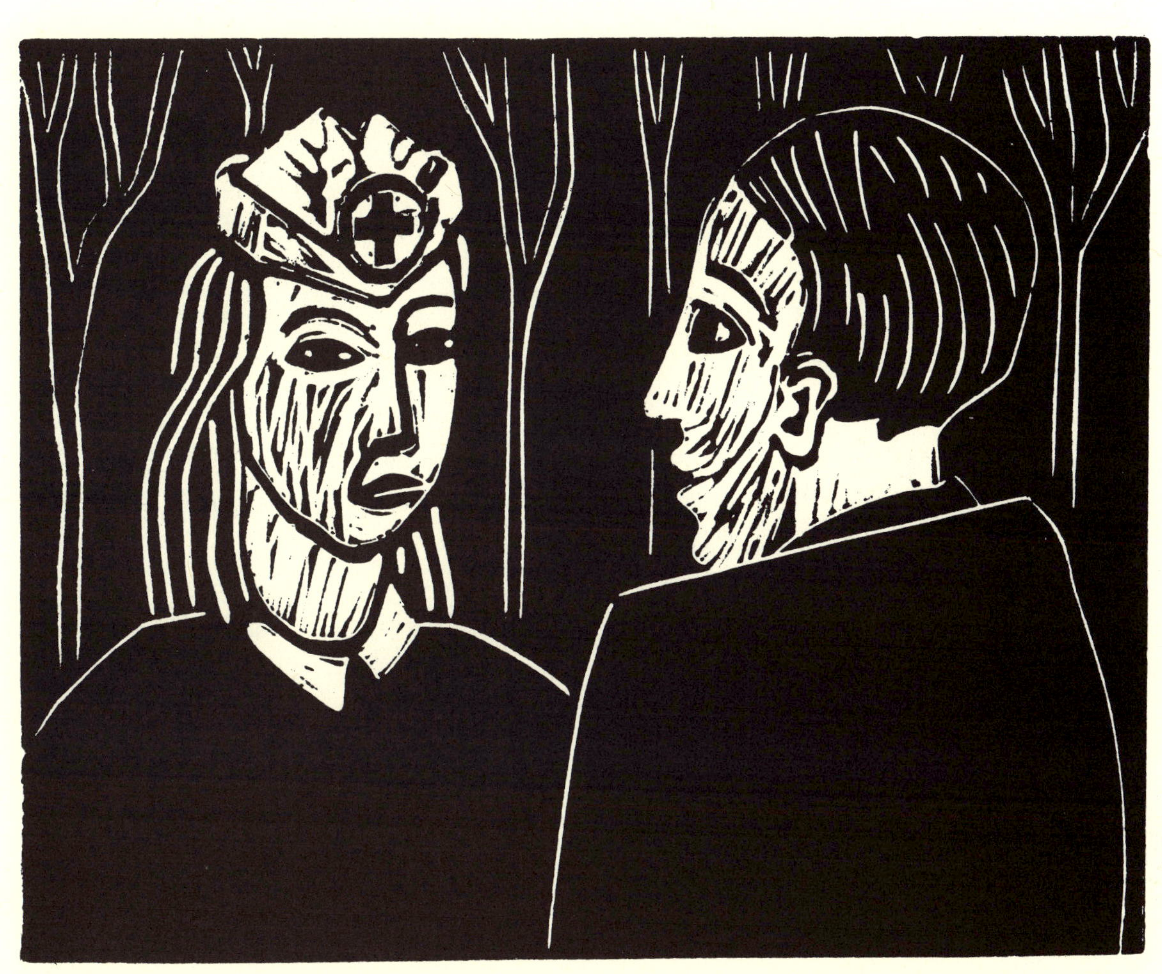

DECEMBER. MY MOTHER, DISGUISED AS A NURSE, WENT TO SEE MY FATHER. SHE PERSUADED HIM TO ESCAPE FROM THE CAMP AND HIDE IN SPAIN. THEN SHE RETURNED TO BRUSSELS AND BEGAN TO PLAN OUR ESCAPE. WE LEFT IN MAY WITHOUT MY GRANDMOTHER. SHE WAS TOO OLD AND LAME TO GO, AND I NEVER SAW HER AGAIN.

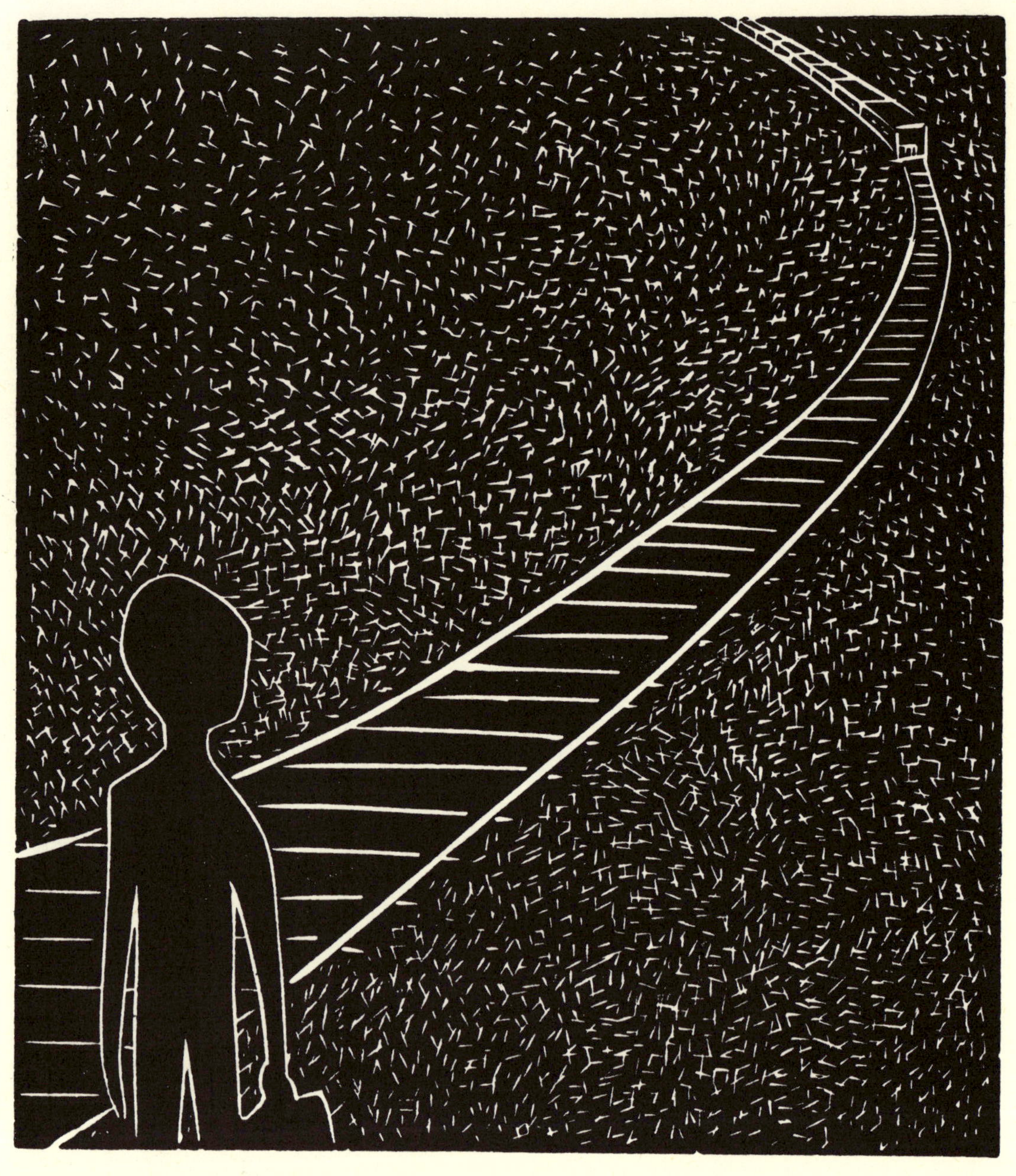

MY MOTHER ARRANGED FOR US TO TRAVEL BY TRAIN WITH A GROUP BEING SMUGGLED TO VICHY FRANCE. BUT AT THE FIRST CHECKPOINT THE GESTAPO FOUND JEWELRY CONCEALED BY A WOMAN TRAVELLING WITH US. WE WERE TAKEN OFF THE TRAIN AND SEARCHED. I WATCHED AS THE TRAIN PULLED OUT OF THE STATION. THEY LET US GO. NOW WE WERE ALL ALONE

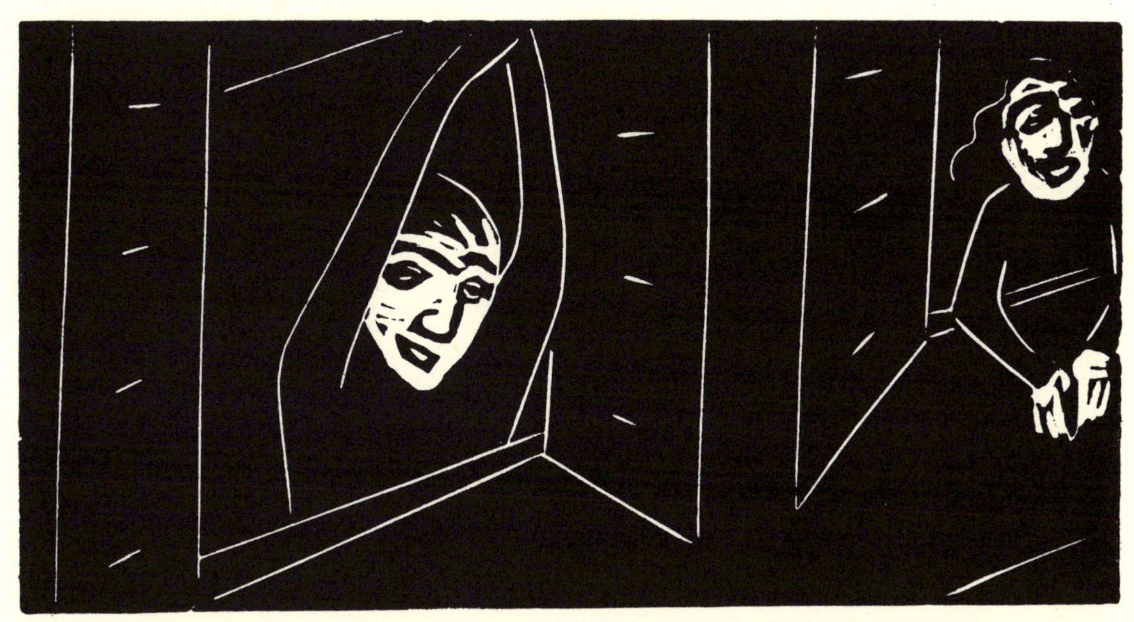

WE GOT BACK ON THE TRAIN THE NEXT DAY. AN OLD MAN HELPED US BRIBE THE ENGINEER TO LET US OFF BEFORE THE CHECKPOINT AT AMIENS. AVOIDING THE GESTAPO, WE GOT ON ANOTHER TRAIN TO PARIS. THERE, DURING AN ALLIED AIR RAID, PARISIANS LEANED OUT THEIR DARKENED WINDOWS AND APPLAUDED. FROM PARIS WE WENT TO VERDELAIS, ON THE VICHY BORDER. I SPENT THE NIGHT WATCHING THE CLOCK AND WORRYING ABOUT ESCAPE.

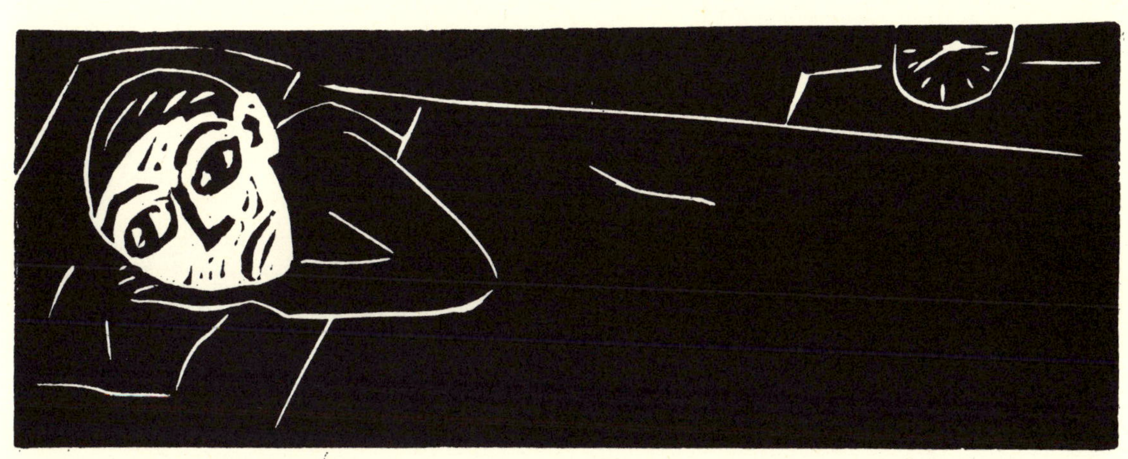

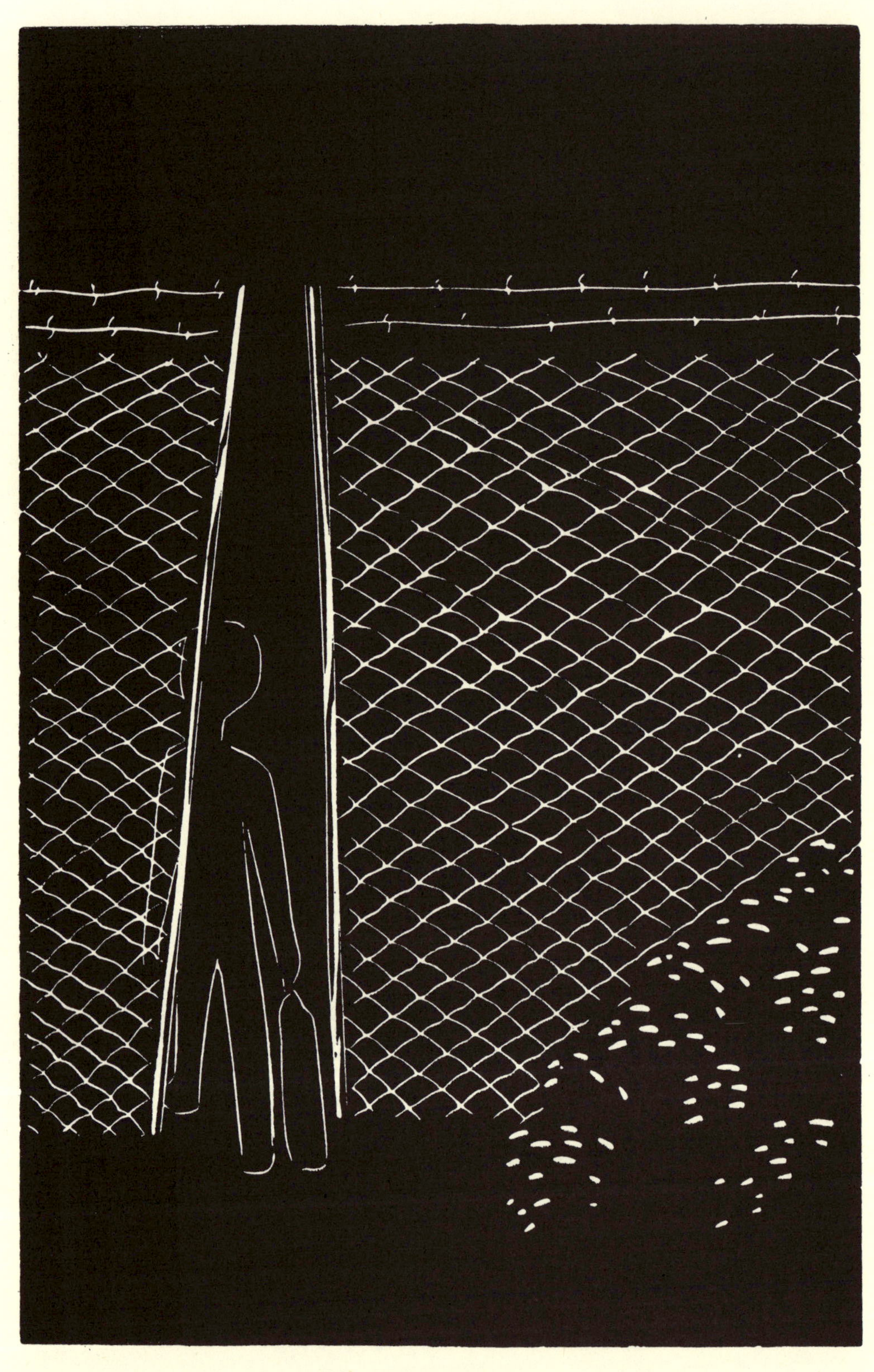

AT 4:30 THE NEXT MORNING WE MET IN A GROUP. SINGLE FILE, WE WALKED SILENTLY THROUGH DARK FIELDS AND WOODS, AND THROUGH A GAP IN THE FENCE AT THE BORDER. WE MET MY FATHER, AND FINALLY WE LEFT EUROPE

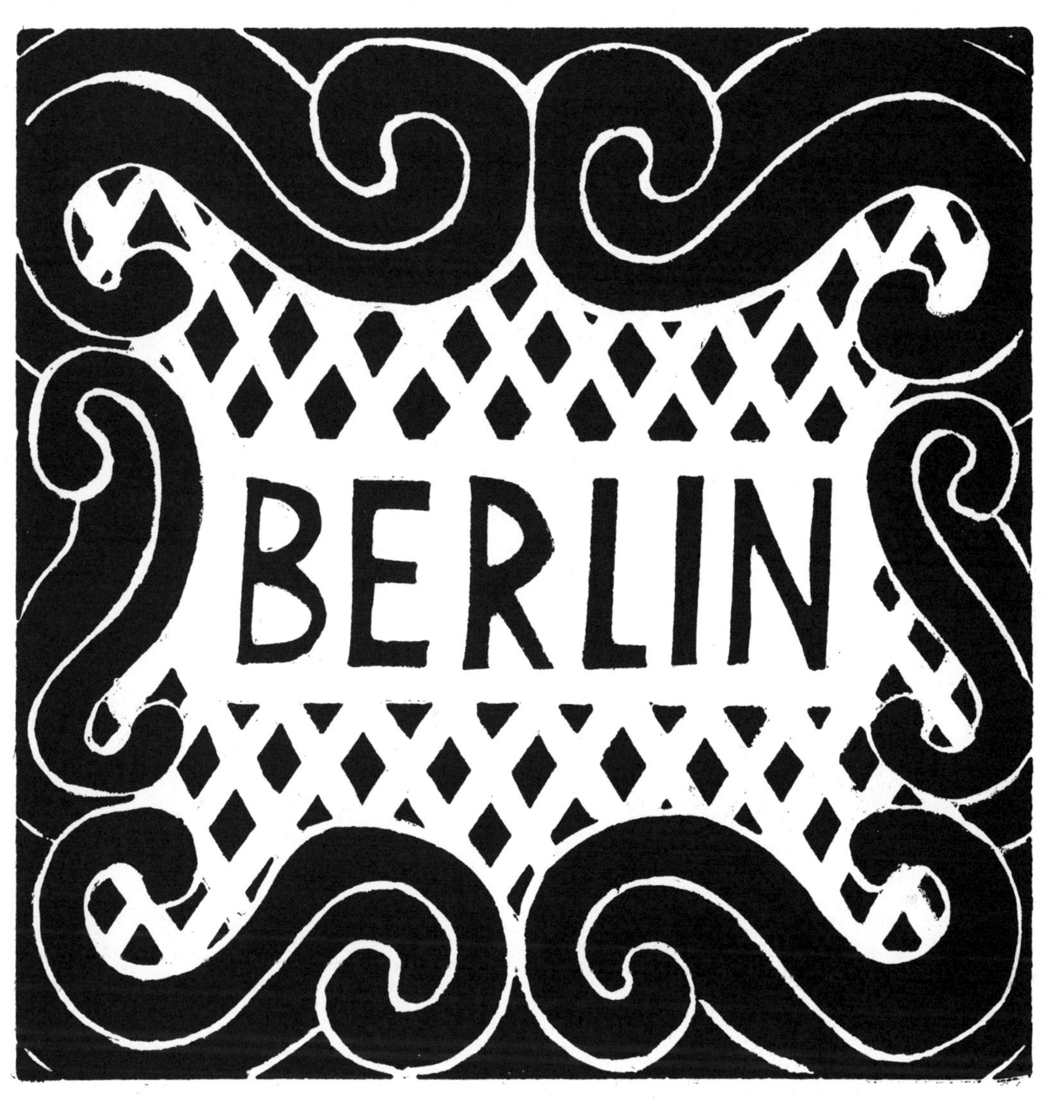
BERLIN

When Hitler came to power in 1933, his private army of storm troopers, known as Brown Shirts or the SA, began a reign of terror against Jews, communists, socialists, trade unionists, and other enemies of the Nazi party. In 1933, there were 400,000 SA members, four times the number of troops allowed to the official German army by the Treaty of Versailles, signed at the conclusion of World War I.

Starting in 1933, the number of Jews permitted in secondary schools and universities was severely limited; Jewish instructors were dismissed. Although students were not expelled from elementary schools in that year, teachers and non-Jewish students created a very hostile environment, resulting in many Jewish students transferring to Jewish schools. It was not until 1938 that Jewish children were prohibited from attending public schools.

Rita Kuhn was born of a Jewish father and a mother who had converted to Judaism after marriage. Rita and her brother were raised as Jews. In 1933, the first legal definition of a Jew (non-Aryan) was enacted: any person with one Jewish parent or one Jewish grandparent was so classified. This definition was refined in 1935, after passage of the Nuremberg Laws, to distinguish between "full Jews" (persons who had at least three grandparents who were "full Jews by race") and *Mischlings* (offspring of mixed marriages, who had one full Jewish parent and one Aryan parent). However, a *Mischling* was treated as a full Jew if, like Rita, the person was a member of the Jewish religious community when the law was enacted in 1935 or if certain other criteria applied.

In 1938, 17,000 Polish Jews were expelled from Germany. Upset by the expulsion of his parents, on November 7, 1938, seventeen-year-old Herschel Grynszpan entered the German embassy in Paris and shot and killed the German third secretary. This shooting was the pretext for the rioting and violence against Jews in Germany that has come to be known as *Kristallnacht* ("The Night of Broken Glass"). On the night of November 9, 1938, over 500 synagogues throughout Germany were burned; 91 Jews were killed; 30,000 Jews were arrested and deported to concentration camps; 7,500 Jewish businesses were destroyed; and millions of dollars worth of Jewish shop windows were shattered. The $10 million in insurance payments for the destroyed Jewish businesses was confiscated by the state, and the Jewish community was fined $400 million.

Many Jews in Germany, including Rita Kuhn and her brother and father, were assigned to forced labor. By 1943, however, the Holocaust was in full operation, and the Nazis sought to remove all Jews from Germany and German-occupied Europe and to send them to extermination camps. Roundups of Jews from factories and businesses were commonplace. Most of these Jews were sent to the camps, but Rita, probably because she was a child of a mixed marriage, was spared.

Since Jews were defined by race, a non-Jew like Rita's mother, who had married a Jew and converted to Judaism, was still considered Aryan and as such not subject to deportation with her family. The demonstration by Christian German wives of Jewish men on Rosenstrasse in March 1943 was one of the few incidents of public resistance to anti-Jewish actions by German citizens. In the face of this resistance, the Nazis backed down and released hundreds of Jewish husbands and children. Rita and her family were among those released, and they were not arrested again for the duration of the war.

After the war, Rita Kuhn remained in Berlin and returned to school. In 1948, she came alone to the United States. Her family remained in Germany.

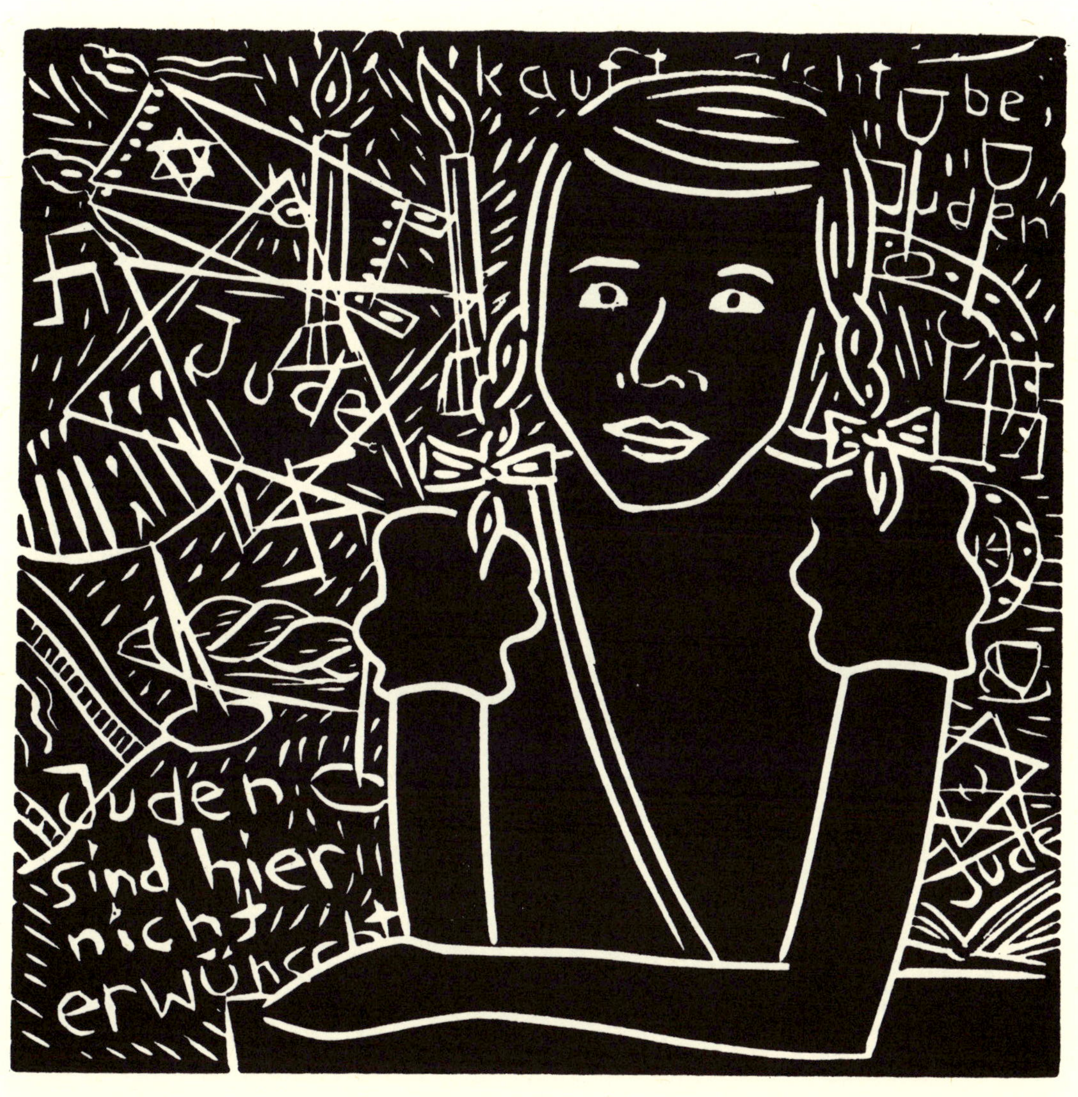

1933. I WAS FIVE YEARS OLD WHEN MY FATHER WARNED ME NOT TO LOOK AT THE MEN IN BROWN UNIFORMS--TO TRY TO BE INVISIBLE. IN FIRST GRADE IN A GERMAN SCHOOL MY TEACHER ASKED US WHO WAS JEWISH. I WAS THE ONLY CHILD WHO RAISED HER HAND. LATER I WAS SENT TO A JEWISH SCHOOL. IT WAS IN OUR SYNAGOGUE. IT FELT SAFE.

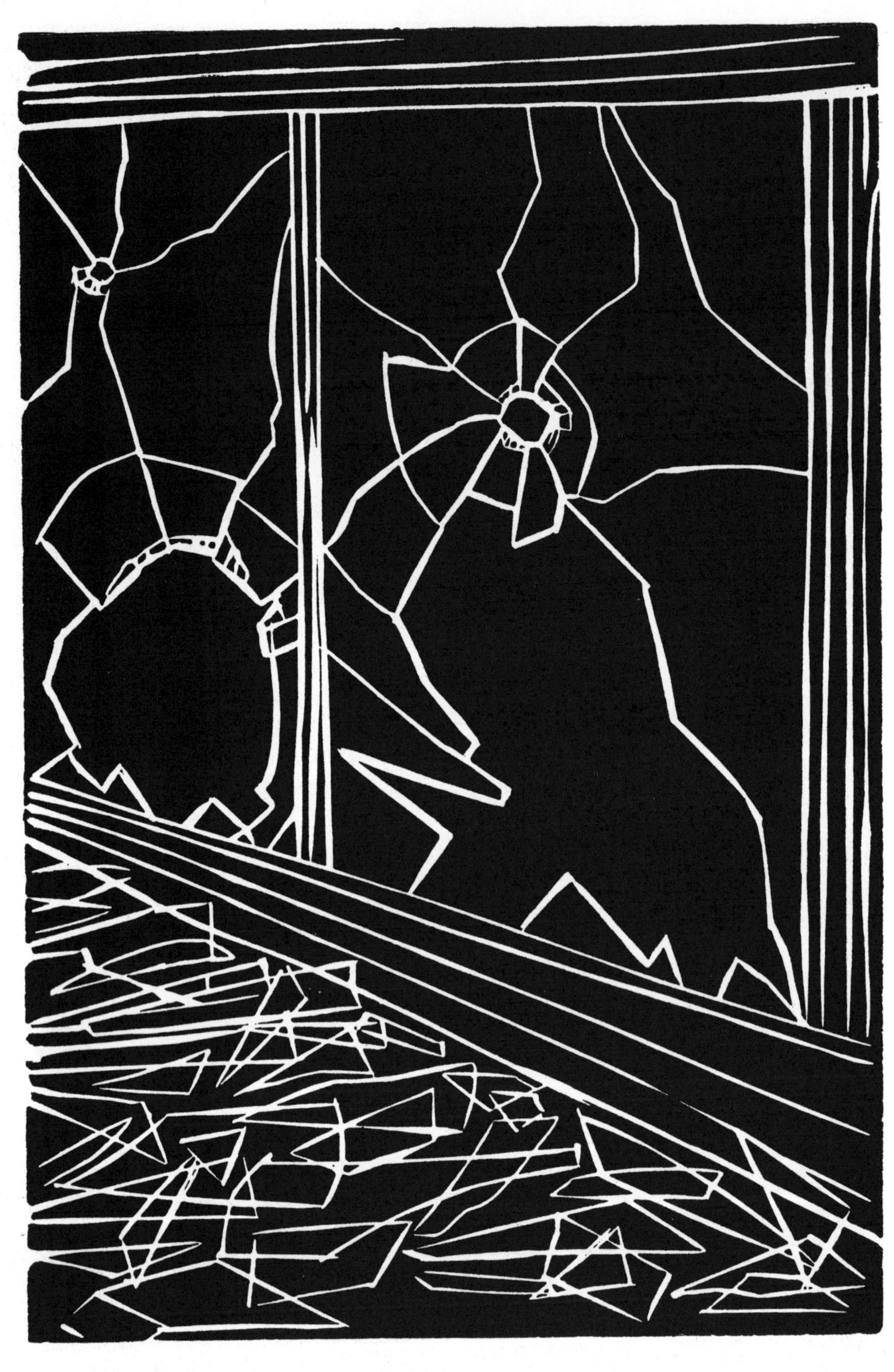

NOVEMBER 10, 1938. GOING TO SCHOOL I SAW SMASHED SHOP WINDOWS. I WAS AFRAID TO LOOK. THE GAPING HOLES, THE DARK, WAS JUST LIKE LOOKING AT DEATH. I DID NOT UNDERSTAND WHAT HAD HAPPENED.

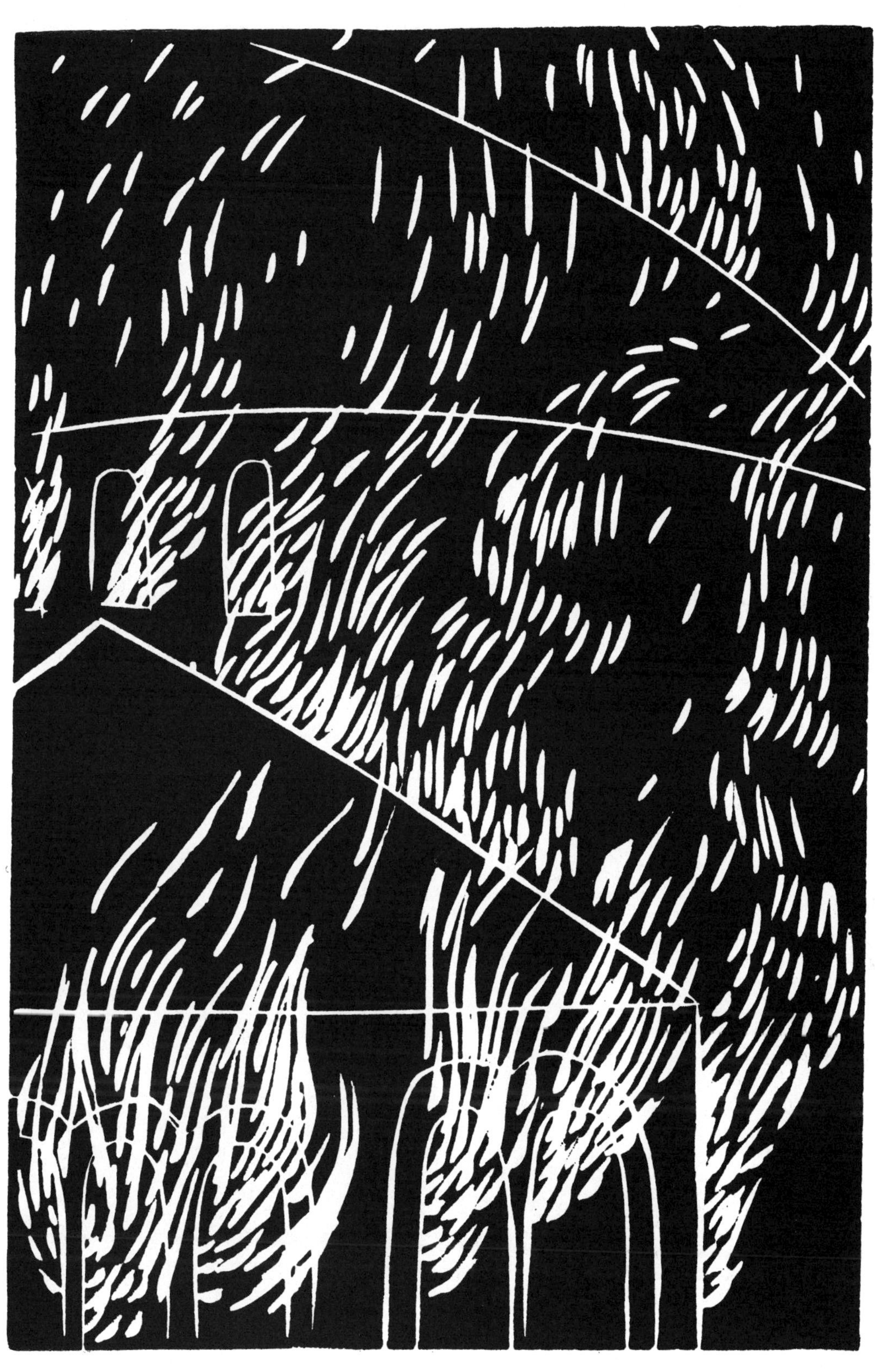

I MET TWO CLASSMATES WHO TOLD ME OUR SCHOOL AND SYNAGOGUE WERE BURNING AND THE BROWN SHIRTS WERE KEEPING THE FIRE TRUCKS FROM PUTTING OUT THE FIRE.

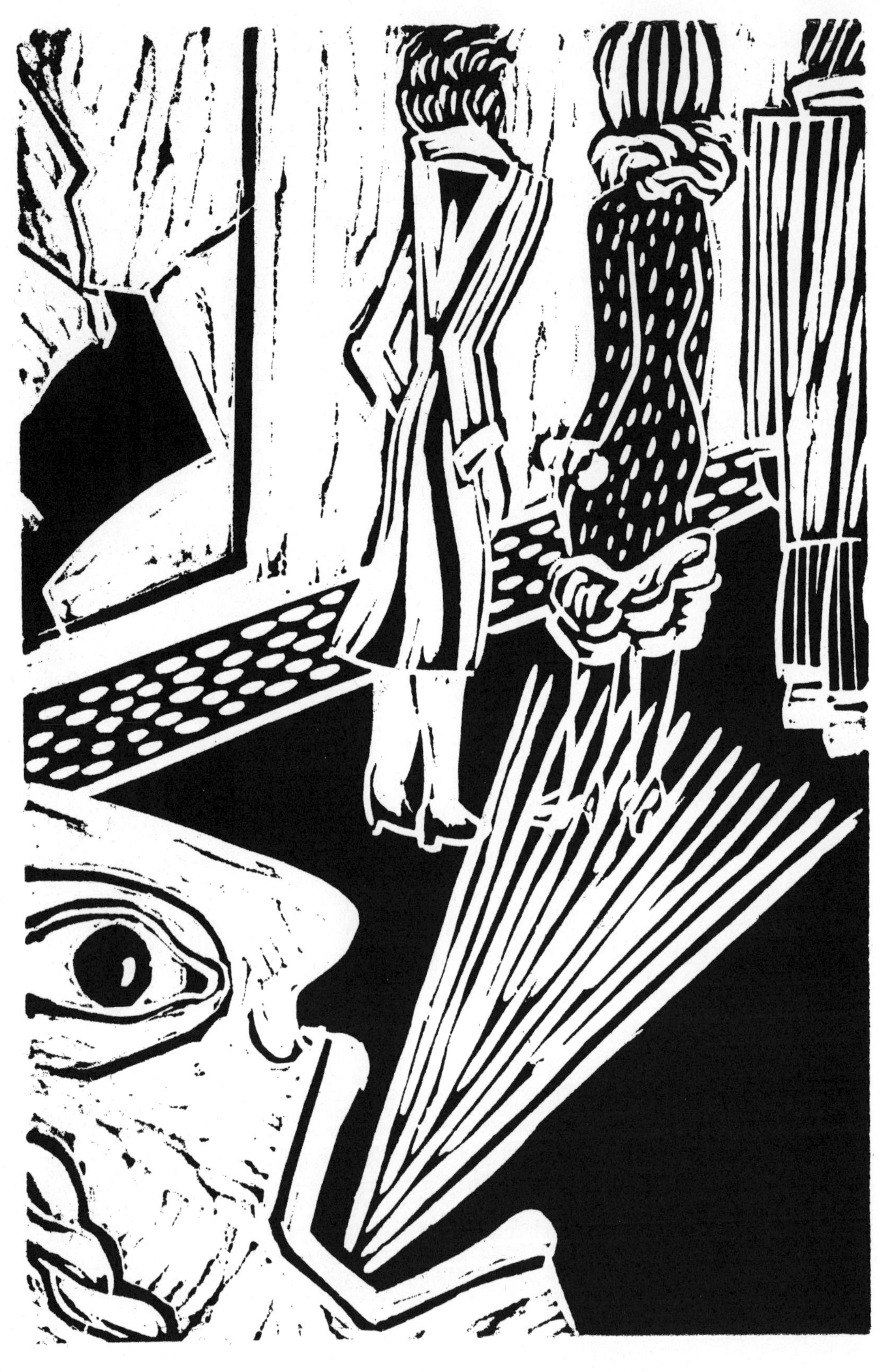

FINALLY I UNDERSTOOD. ENRAGED AND SADDENED, I SCREAMED AT THE PASSERSBY, BUT THEY TURNED AWAY.

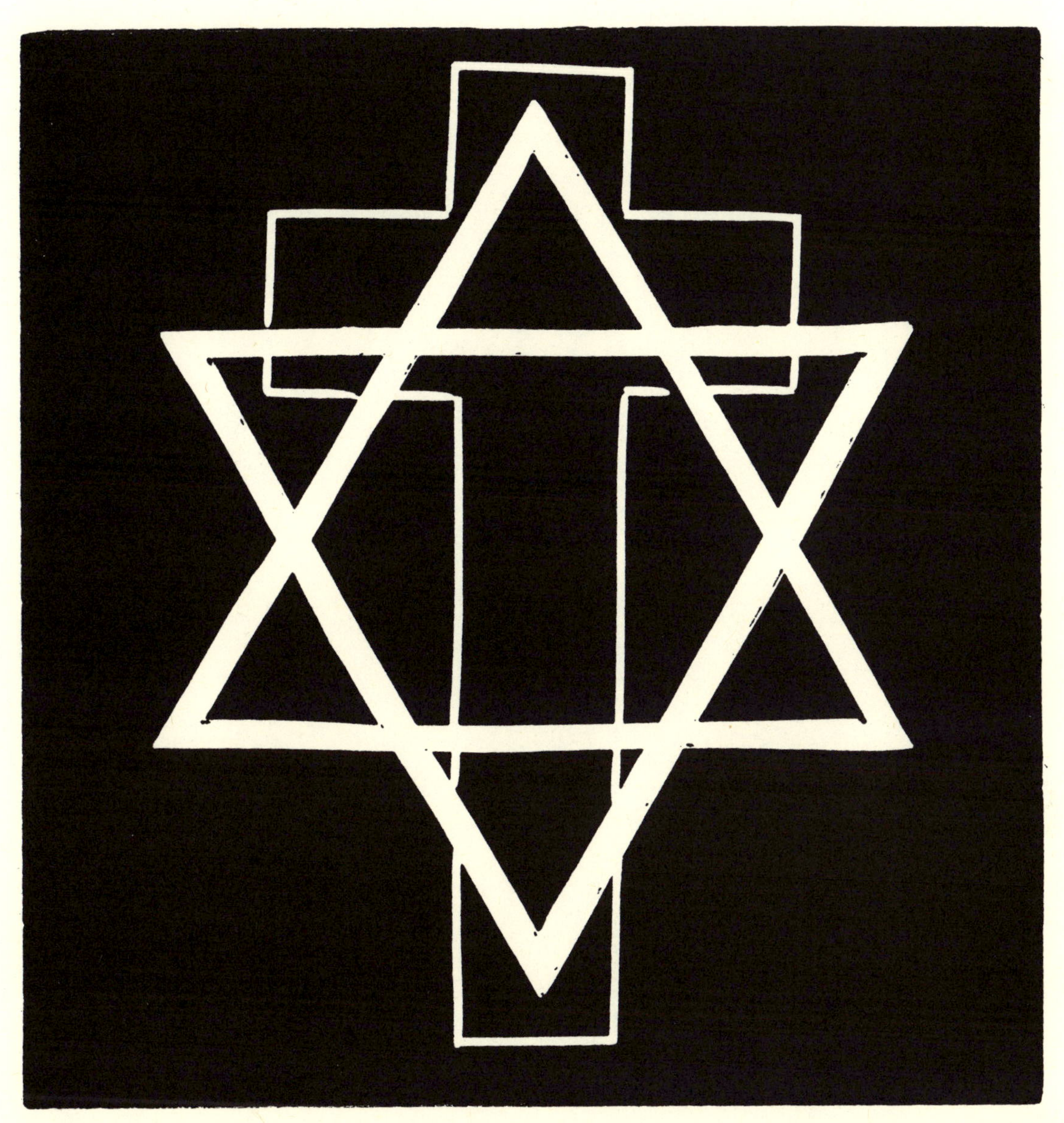

1939. MY FATHER INSISTED THAT I BE BAPTIZED. I OBJECTED, "IF I HAVE TO DIE, I'LL DIE AS A JEW. GOD WILL PUNISH ME IF I LEAVE MY FAITH!" FATHER SAID "GOD WILL FORGIVE YOU!" BUT I PRAYED THE BAPTISM WOULD NOT WORK. WHEN THE NAZIS MADE ME WEAR THE YELLOW STAR EVEN THOUGH I HAD BEEN BAPTIZED, I FELT THAT GOD HAD HEARD MY PRAYER.

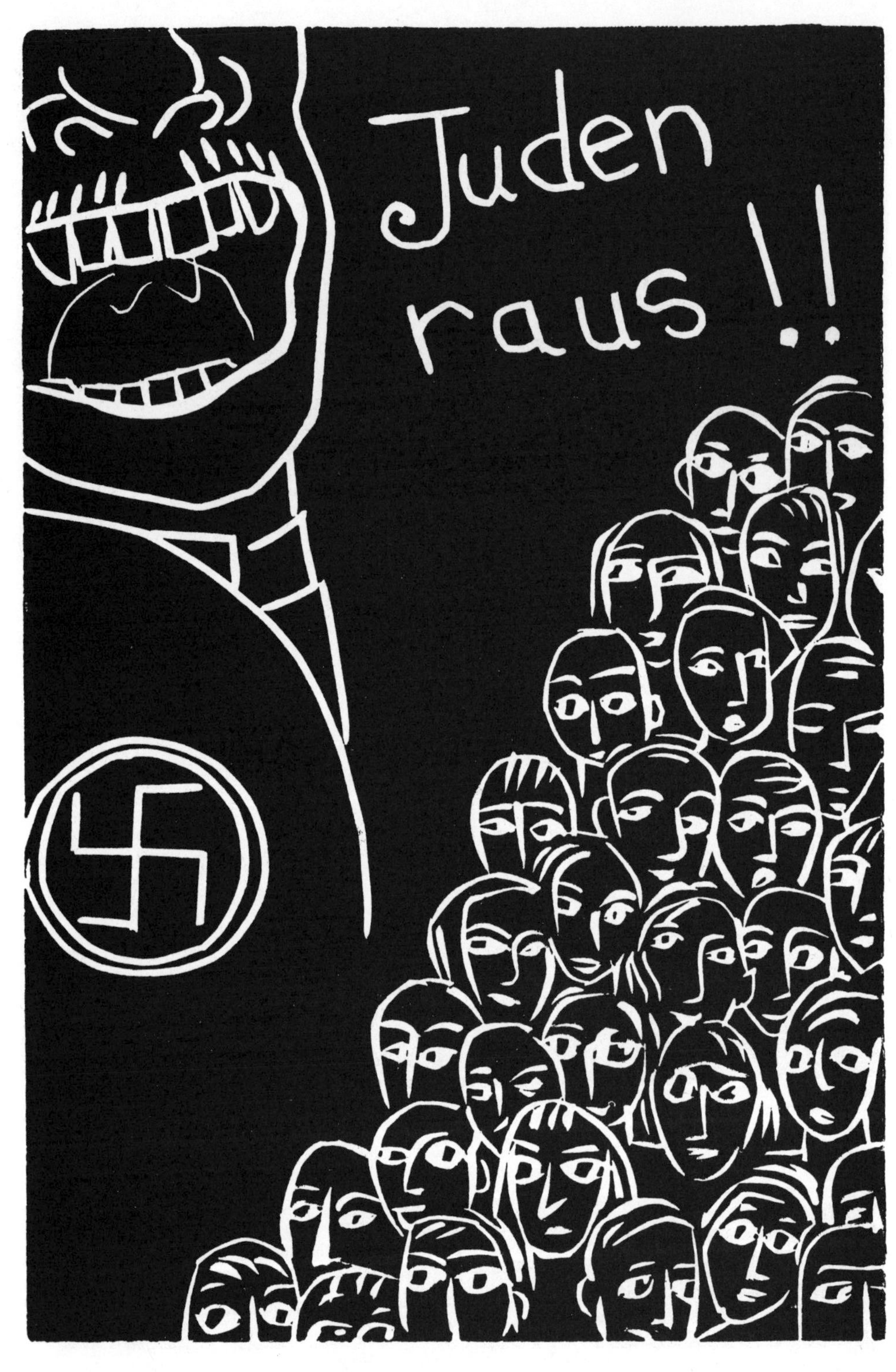

FEBRUARY 27, 1943. THE SS CAME TO THE FACTORY AND SCREAMED "JEWS OUT!" WE WERE LOADED IN TRUCKS. IT WAS COMPLETELY DARK INSIDE. I WAS AFRAID THE SS WOULD BLOW UP THE TRUCKS.

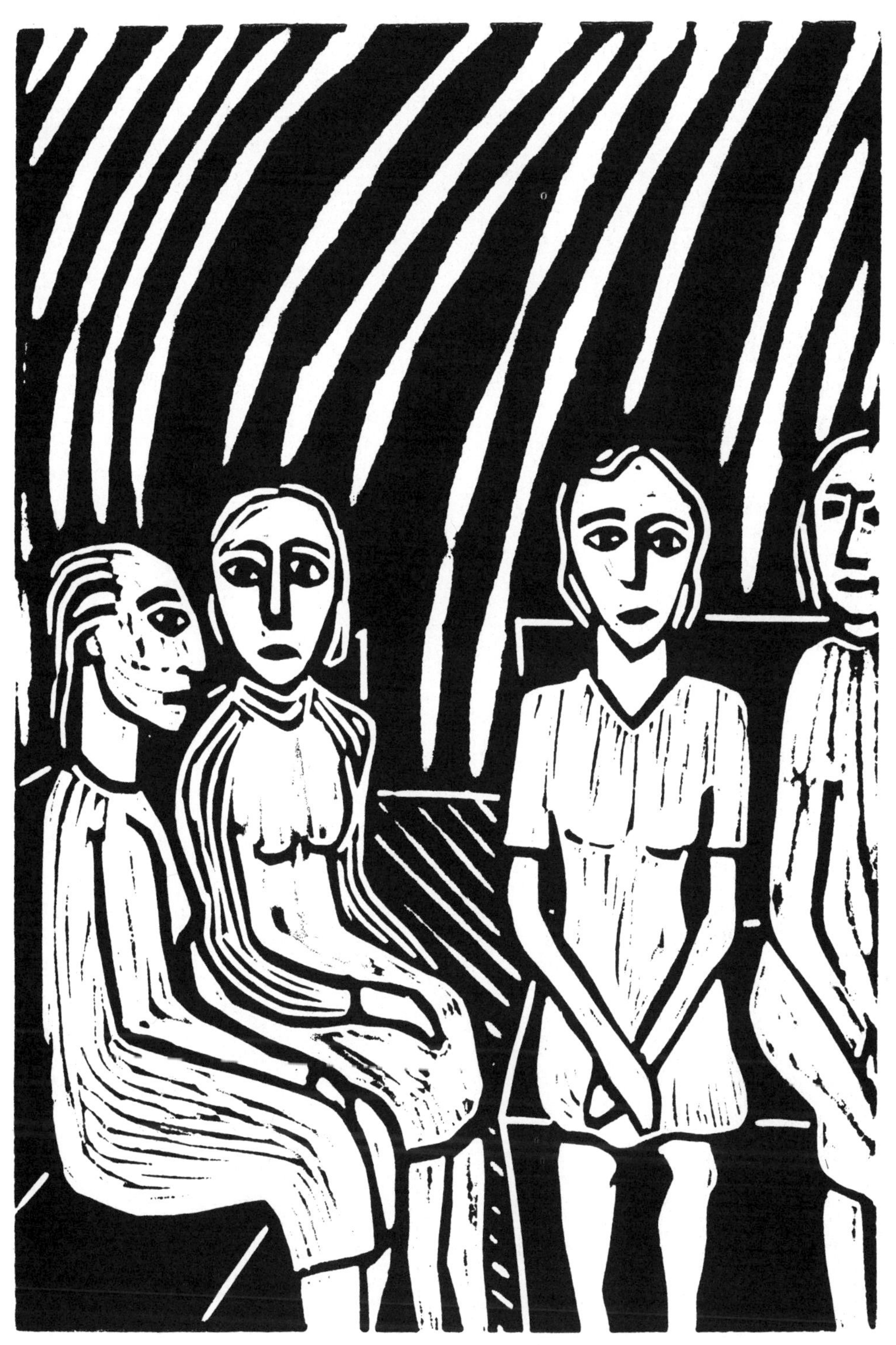

THEY TOOK US TO A LARGE DANCE HALL. ALL DAY MORE WOMEN CAME. WE HAD NOTHING TO EAT OR DRINK. IT WAS VERY QUIET, NO ONE CRIED OR TALKED MUCH. AT ABOUT 10 PM THE SS FINALLY CALLED MY NAME.

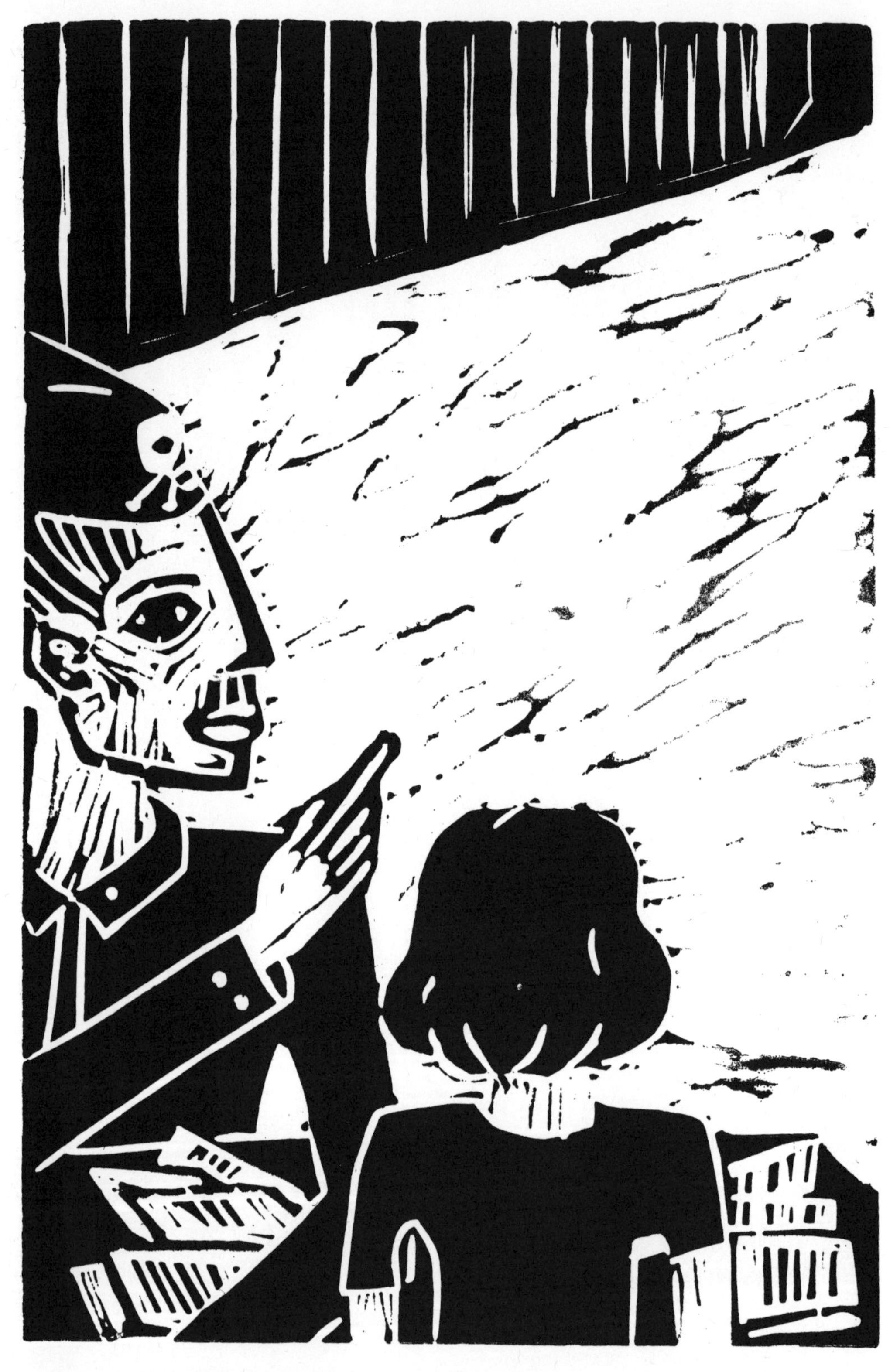

THE SS WERE SENDING MOST OF THE WOMEN OUT A DOOR TO THE LEFT. I KNEW THEY WOULD NEVER RETURN BUT I WAS SENT TO THE DOOR ON THE RIGHT. I STEPPED OUT TO THE DARK SILENCE AND WENT HOME.

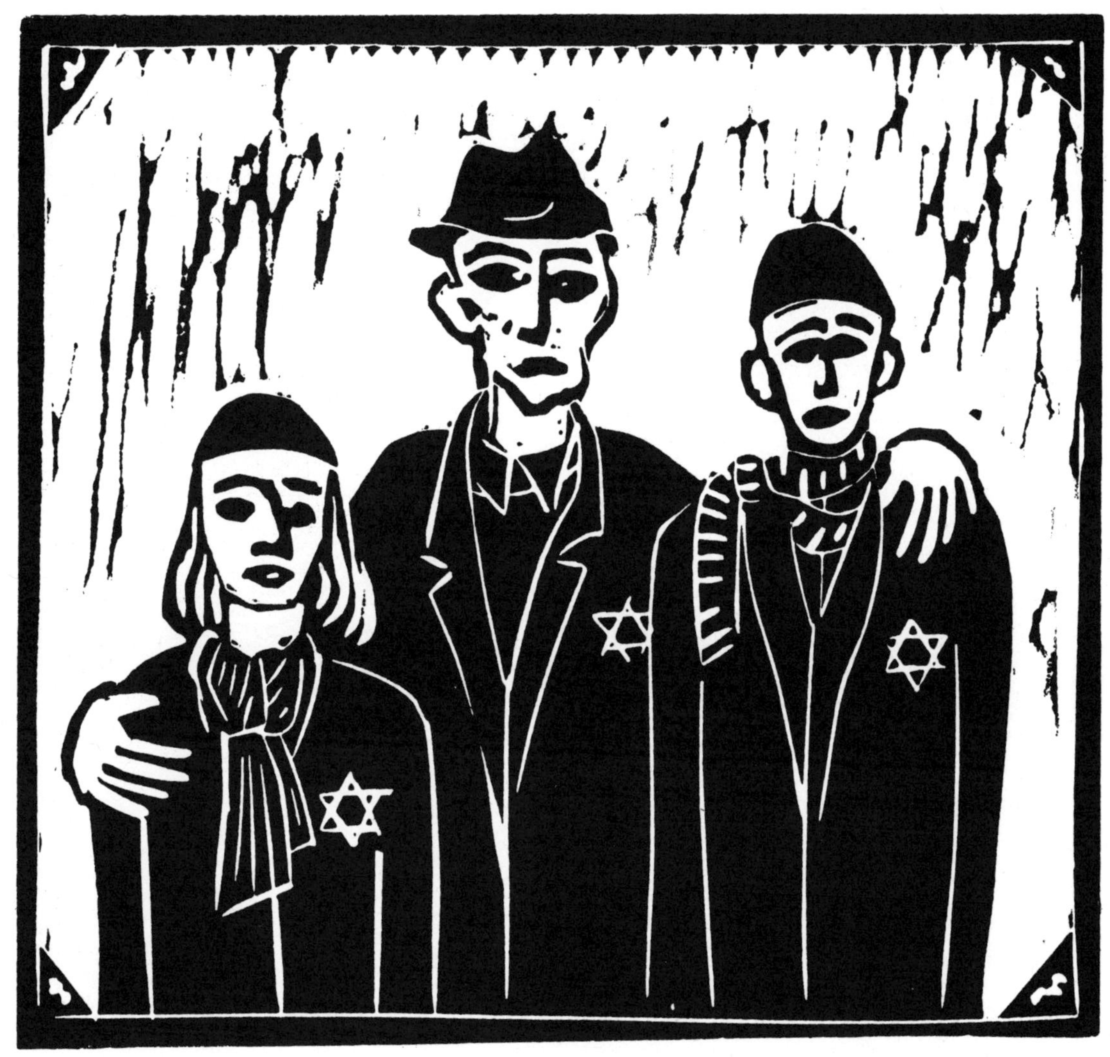

A WEEK LATER MY MOTHER WENT TO GET OUR RATION CARDS; THEY SAID WE HAD TO COME IN PERSON. WHEN MY FATHER, BROTHER AND I WENT FOR OUR CARDS THE SS PUT US IN A BIG ROOM. DURING THE DAY, ALL THE OTHER JEWS IN THE AREA WERE BROUGHT IN. MY MOTHER WAS NOT JEWISH, SO SHE COULD NOT STAY WITH US. ALL DAY I HEARD HER SCREAM OUTSIDE THE ROOM, "I WANT TO BE WITH MY CHILDREN."

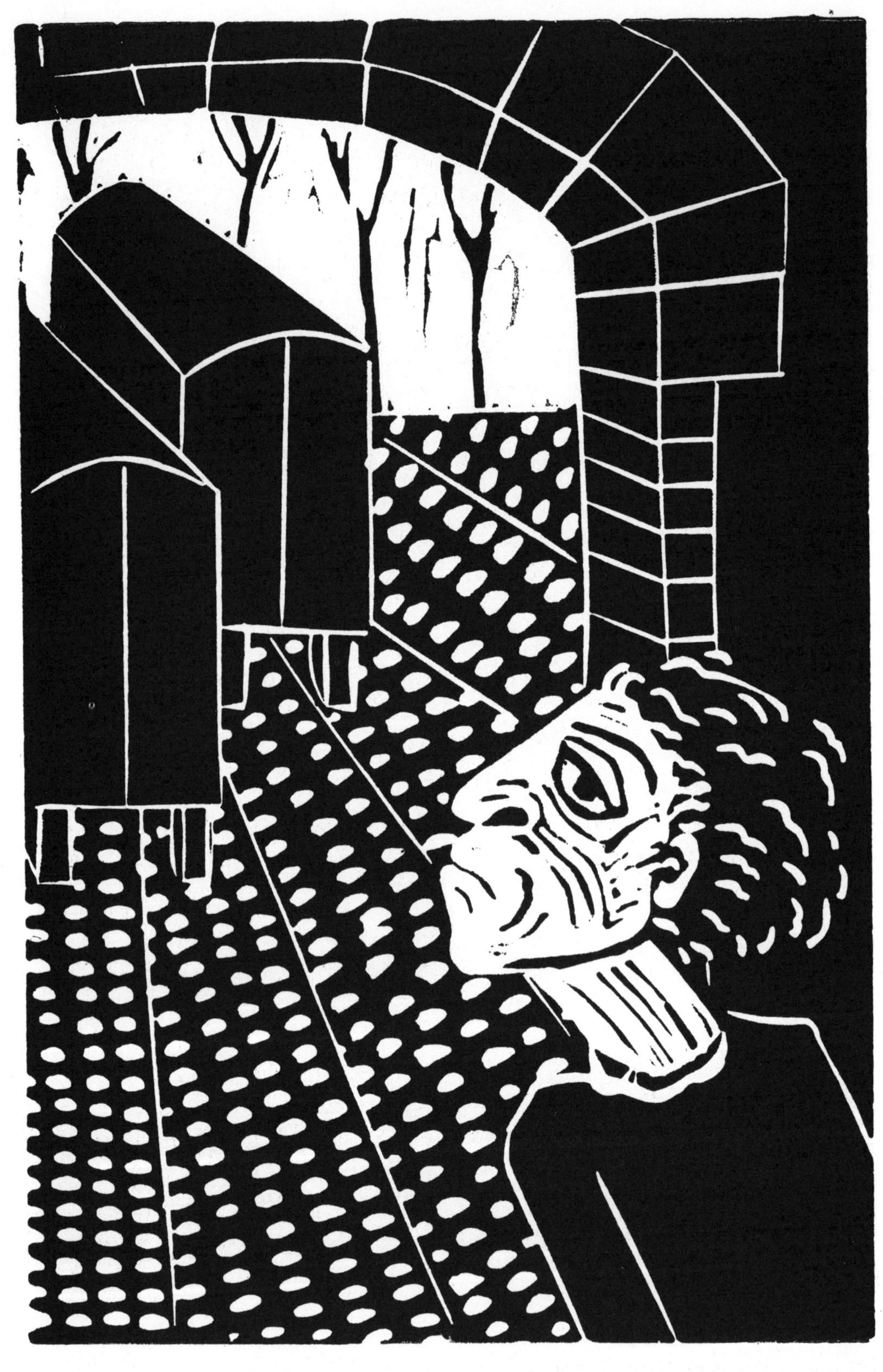

IN THE EVENING THE SS TOOK US AWAY IN TRUCKS. MY MOTHER WATCHED FROM THE DOORWAY, SILENT AND STILL, AS WE LEFT.

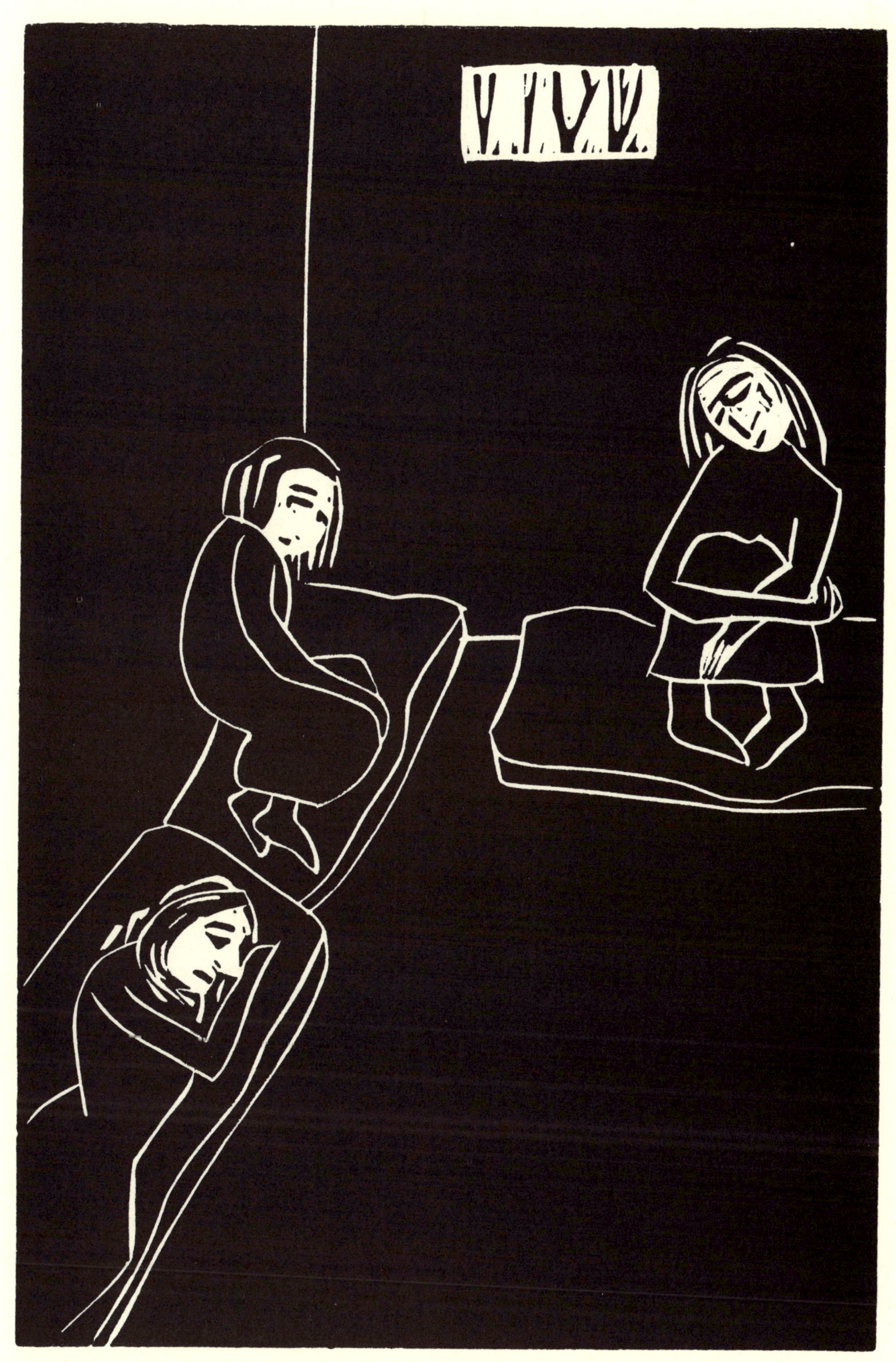

WE WERE TAKEN TO A BUILDING ON ROSENSTRASSE. THERE I WAS SEPARATED FROM MY FATHER AND BROTHER. I WAS PUT IN A SMALL, DARK ROOM WITH A HIGH WINDOW AND THREE OTHER WOMEN.

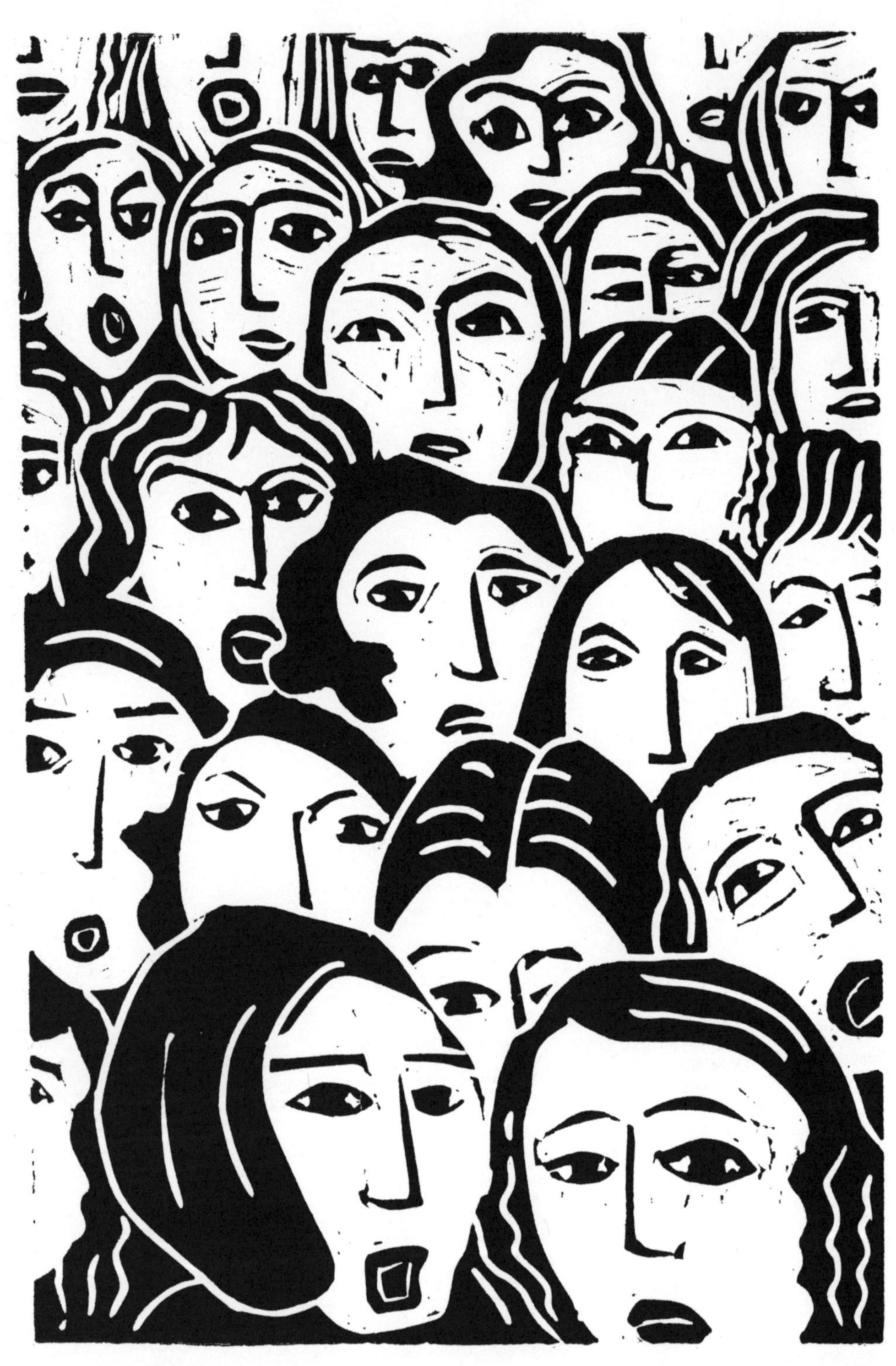

OUTSIDE HUNDREDS OF CHRISTIAN WIVES OF JEWISH HUSBANDS HAD DEMONSTRATED ALL WEEK, YELLING "GIVE US BACK OUR MEN!" FINALLY THE SS RELEASED THE JEWS FROM ROSENSTRASSE AND WE WENT HOME.

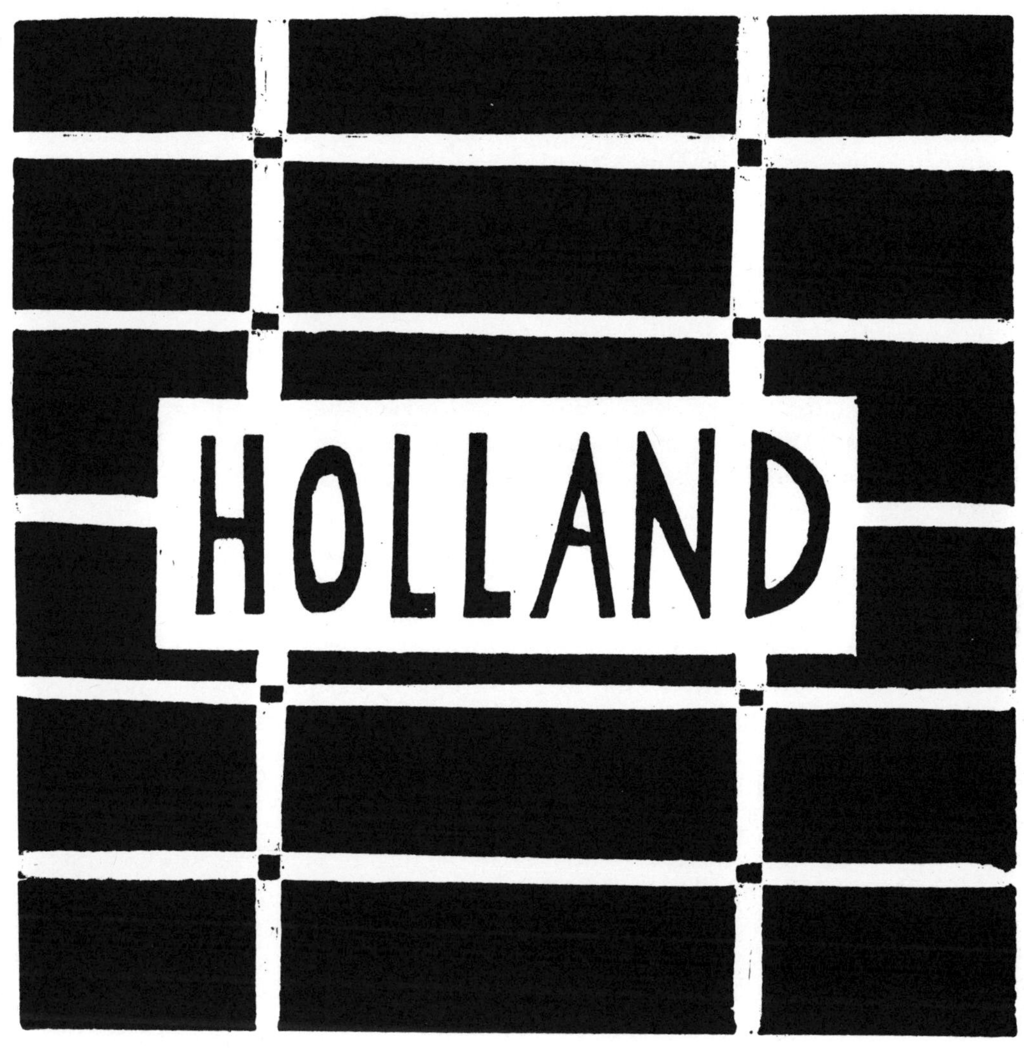
HOLLAND

Holland was invaded by the Germans on May 10, 1940. The Dutch, following an unsuccessful attempt to stop the German advance by evacuating the population and flooding the lowlands, surrendered after only five days. The Dutch royal family and government fled to England; the remaining government officials collaborated with the occupying Nazi military command. Measures to identify and restrict the activities of Jews were instituted in September 1940, and although the Dutch government-in-exile did not protest the anti-Jewish measures, most of the Catholic and Protestant churches offered public condemnations. The Dutch underground worked with the Dutch churches in resisting the Nazis and helping the Jews.

At the time of the German invasion there were 140,000 Jews in Holland, and by the summer of 1943 the Germans estimated that there were approximately 20,000 Dutch Jews in hiding. About 18,000 of the hidden Jews survived the war, including at least two of the three Jews hidden by **Hielke Sheneman** and her family. Holland had more "righteous gentiles" than any other European country. By 1990 over 3,200 Dutch citizens had been honored by the State of Israel for helping Jews escape the Holocaust, often by hiding them from the Nazis.

Despite the heroic efforts of "righteous gentiles," Dutch Jews were continually in danger. The Nazis frequently conducted *Aktions* in which they systematically rounded up Jews for deportation. In just one *Aktion* in Amsterdam in June 1943, 5,500 Jews were netted. A total of over 107,000 (75%) of the Dutch Jews were deported to death camps, where almost all (95%) perished. Less than one quarter of the Dutch Jews survived the war, the survival rate of Jews in Holland being one of the lowest in Western Europe.

Toward the end of the war, food shortages were severe in German-occupied Holland, where an estimated 16,000 Dutch civilians died of starvation. The Allied Forces launched a program of relief efforts. One documented example, perhaps the incident described by Hielke Sheneman, took place on April 29, 1945, when Britain conducted Operation Manna, in which 3,000 bombers dropped food packages behind enemy lines in Holland. In 1943 and 1944, the Red Cross was also active in supplying food to prisoners in concentration camps.

The Dutch resistance continued until the end of the war, and Holland was liberated on May 6, 1945. After the war, Hielke Sheneman stayed in Amsterdam with her family. She worked as a teacher there until 1952, when she joined her sister in the United States.

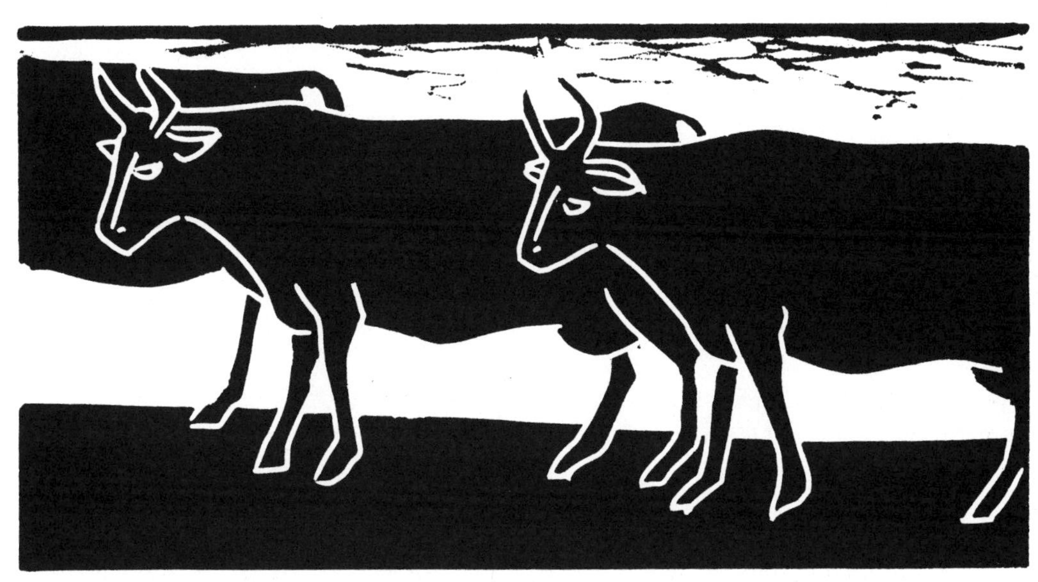

ON MAY 10, 1940, THE GERMANS INVADED HOLLAND. FIRST THE FARM ANIMALS WERE EVACUATED, THEN THE PEOPLE WERE MOVED TO TOWNS ON HIGHER GROUND, AND OUR TOWN WAS INUNDATED. BUT FLOODING DID NOT STOP THE GERMANS. OUR WAR LASTED ONLY FIVE DAYS. AFTER OUR SURRENDER WE WERE SENT HOME TO LIVE UNDER THE GERMAN OCCUPATION.

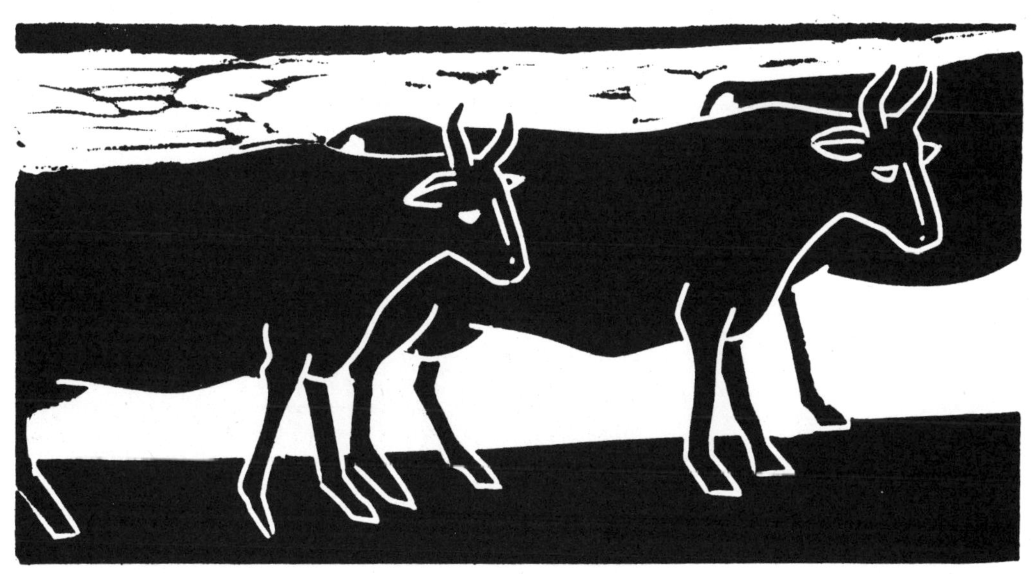

THE FIRST TIME I SAW A NAZI SOLDIER I RAN HOME IN TERROR. I DREAMT NIGHT AFTER NIGHT ABOUT WHAT THEY WOULD DO.

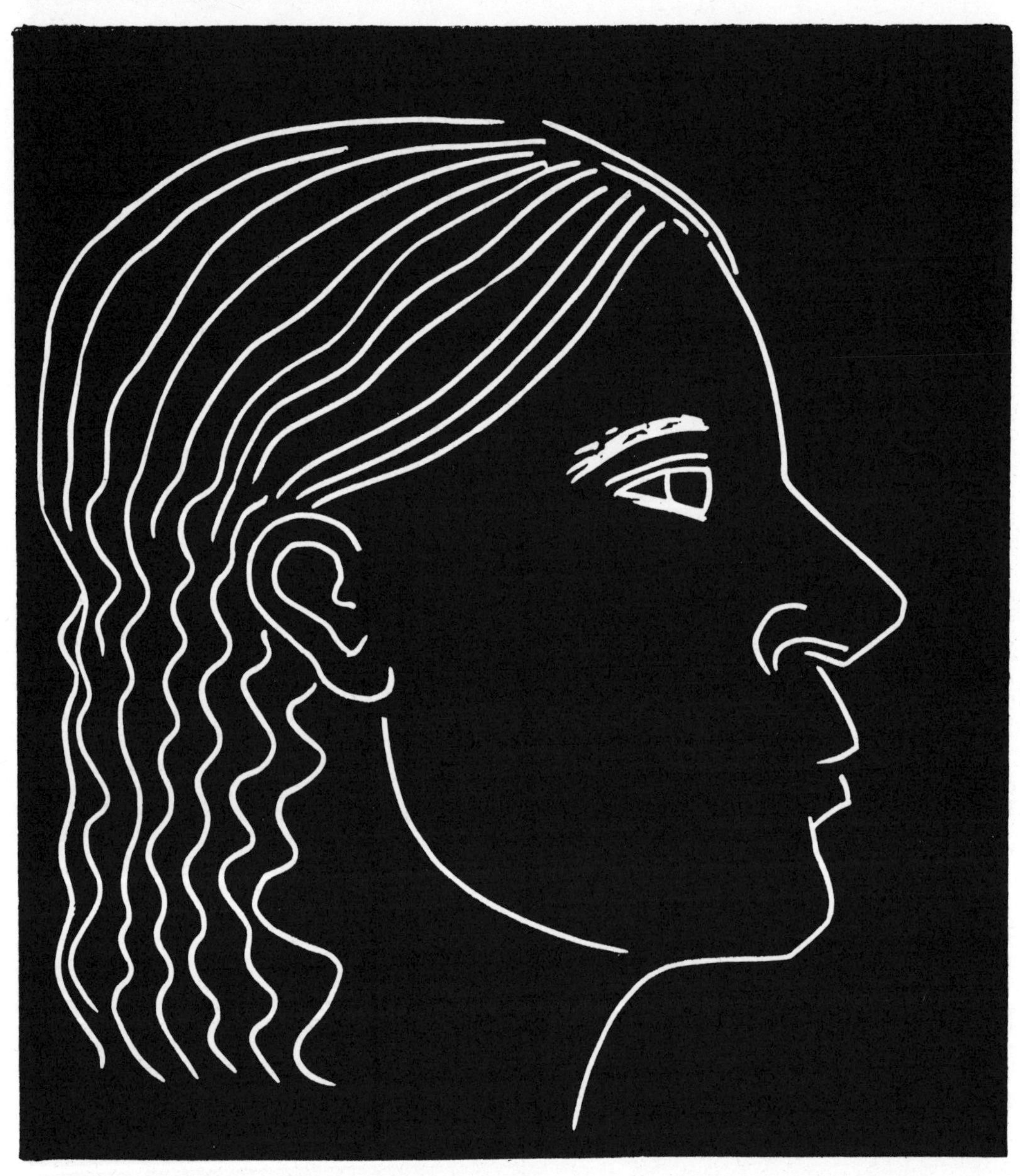

THE GERMANS MADE US CARRY IDENTITY CARDS. THEY TOOK OUR PHOTOGRAPHS IN PROFILE, HAIR PULLED BACK BEHIND THE EARS, TO DETERMINE IF WE WERE JEWISH.

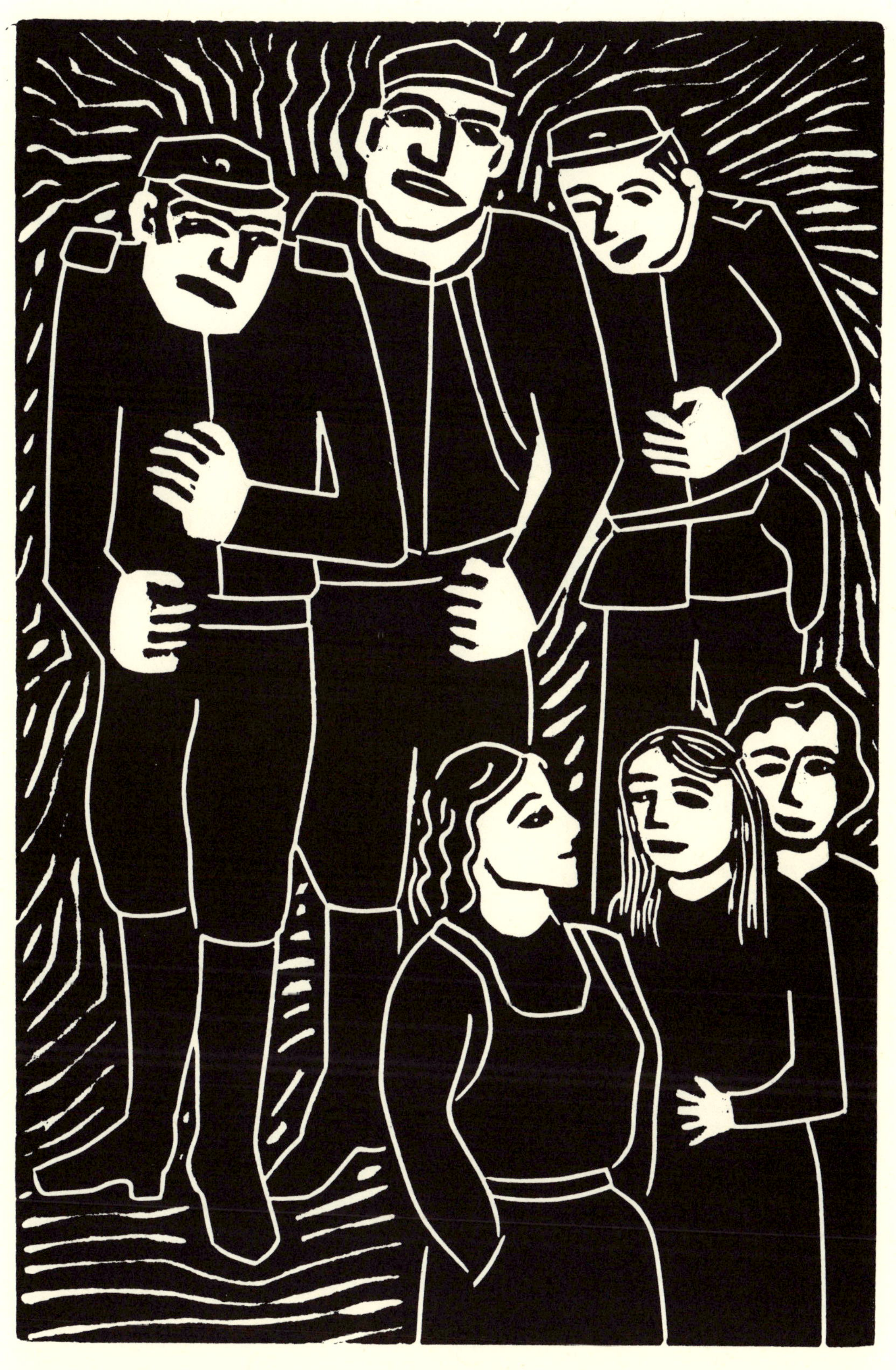

WE WERE SCARED AND DEFIANT. ON THE STREETS WE TURNED OUR BACKS ON THE SOLDIERS AND WE FELT VERY BRAVE.

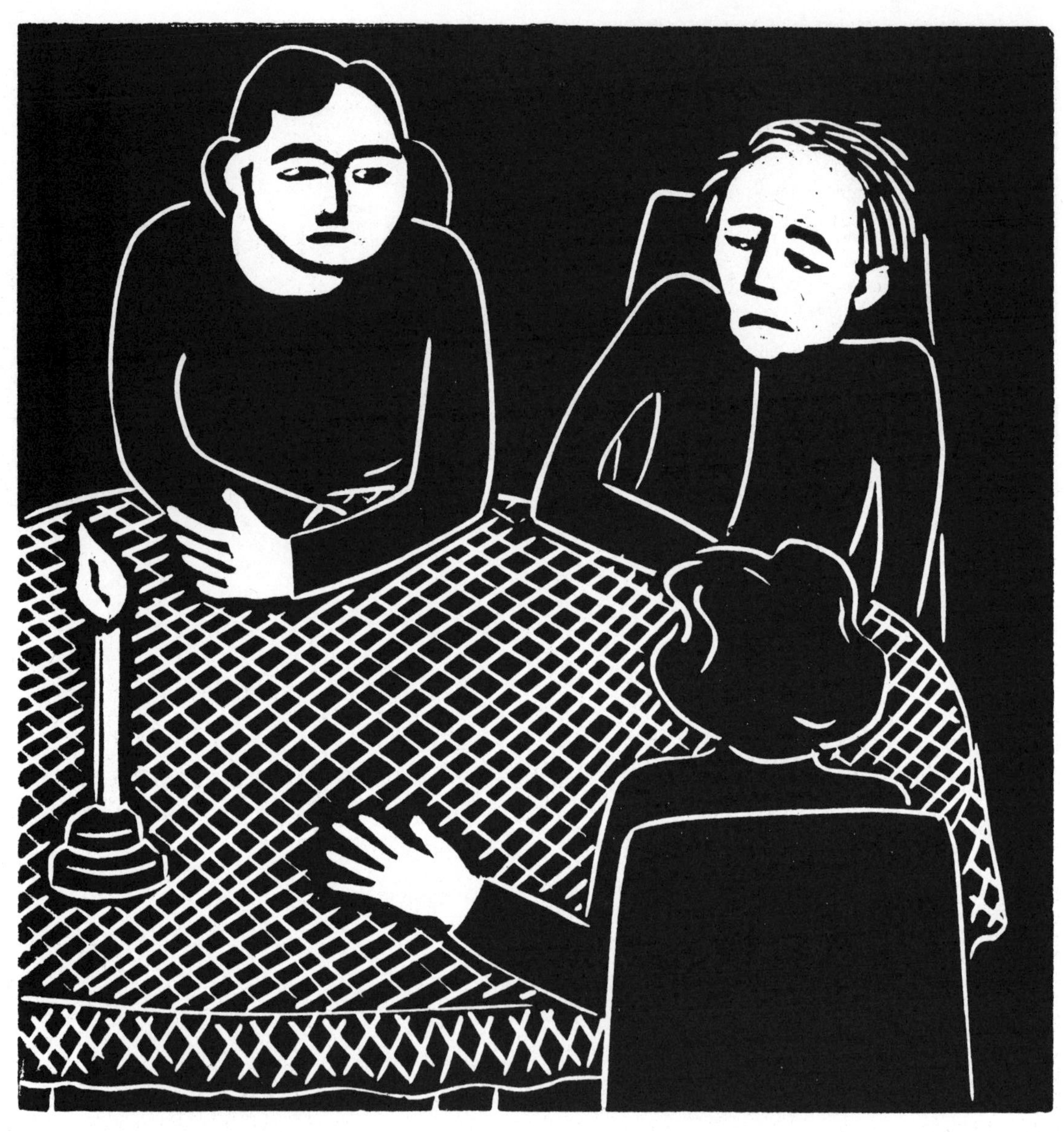

WE WERE CALVINISTS, AND WE WERE VERY SERIOUS ABOUT OUR RELIGIOUS DUTIES. AT HOME WE DISCUSSED WHETHER IT COULD EVER BE RIGHT TO TAKE A LIFE. MY FAMILY THOUGHT IT ALWAYS WAS WRONG TO KILL, BUT IT WAS A DIFFICULT DECISION. WE KNEW THAT LEADERS OF THE UNDERGROUND HAD KILLED NAZIS. YET THEY WERE HEROES.

I MOVED TO AMSTERDAM, WHERE I JOINED THE UNDERGROUND. AT NIGHT I CARRIED MESSAGES AND DELIVERED THE UNDERGROUND NEWSPAPER. IN THE DARK, AFTER THE CURFEW, I WAS ALWAYS VERY SCARED. SOME OF MY FRIENDS WERE CAUGHT AND KILLED, BUT THE GERMANS NEVER SAW ME.

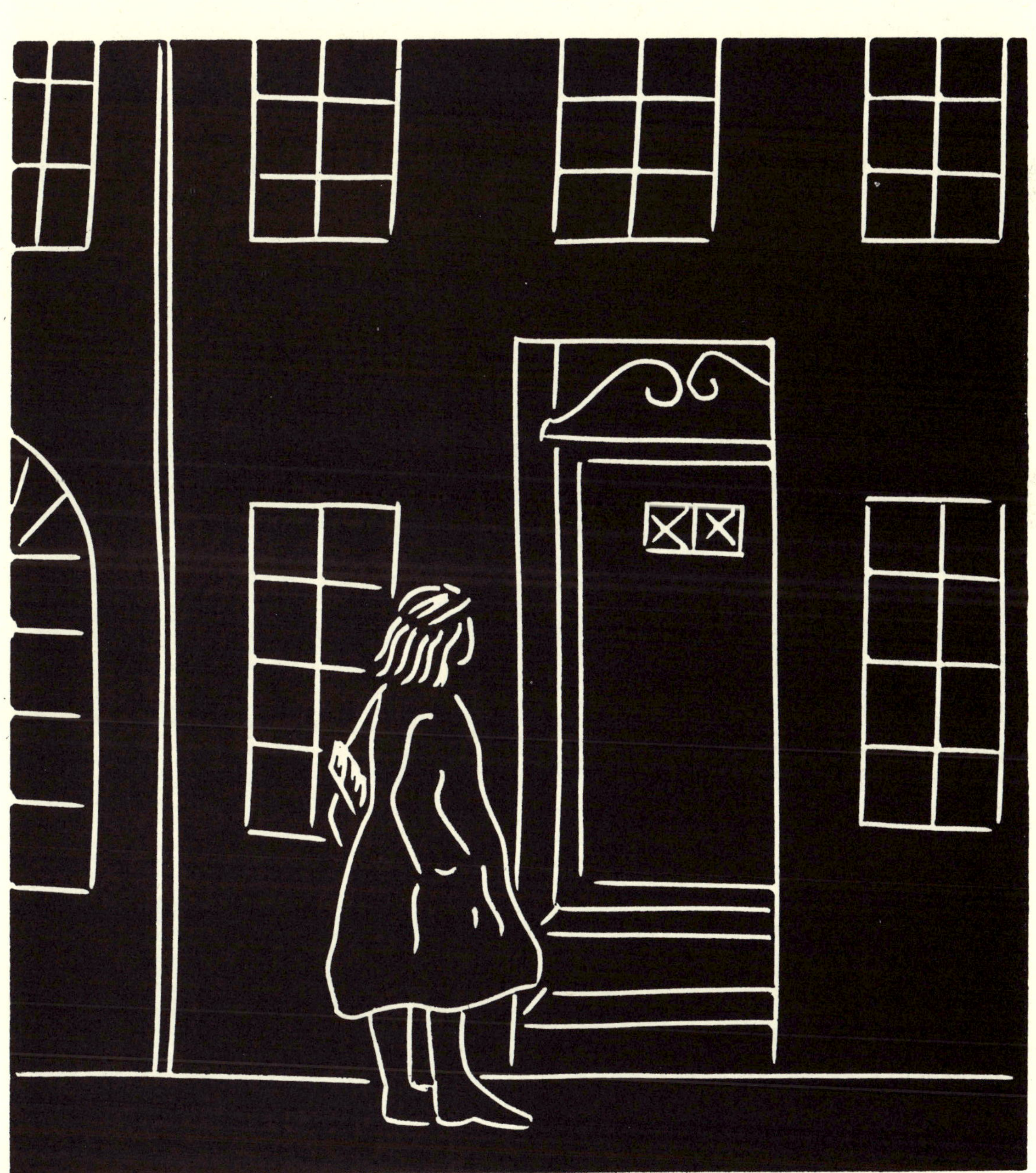

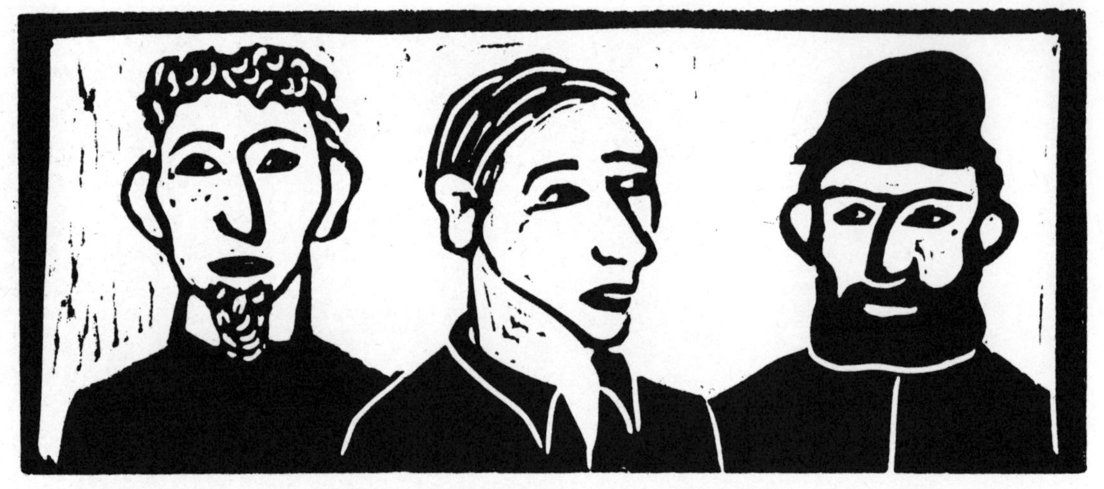

THE UNDERGROUND ASKED US TO HIDE THREE JEWS IN OUR HOUSE. MY FATHER AGREED, AND BUILT A DOUBLE WALL IN THE BASEMENT WHERE THEY COULD HIDE. WHEN WE WERE WARNED OF DANGER THEY HID BEHIND THE WALL. THE REST OF THE TIME THEY STAYED INSIDE THE HOUSE WHERE THEY COULD NOT BE SEEN. THEY LIVED WITH US FOR THREE YEARS. I WAS RESPONSIBLE FOR GETTING EXTRA FOOD FOR THEM.

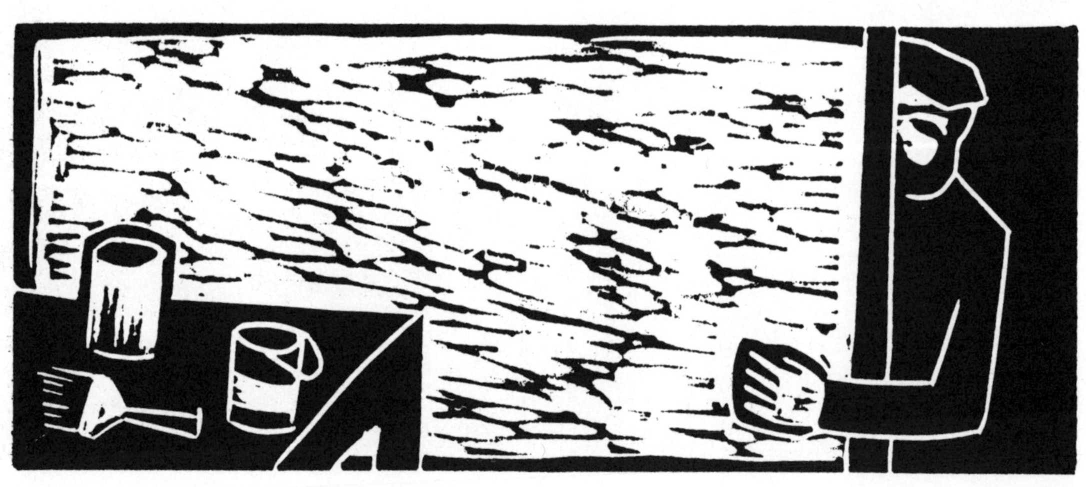

MY BICYCLE HAD ROPE INSTEAD OF TIRES. I RODE IT TO SEARCH FOR FOOD TO BUY--POTATOES, OR SUGAR BEETS, EVEN TULIP BULBS.

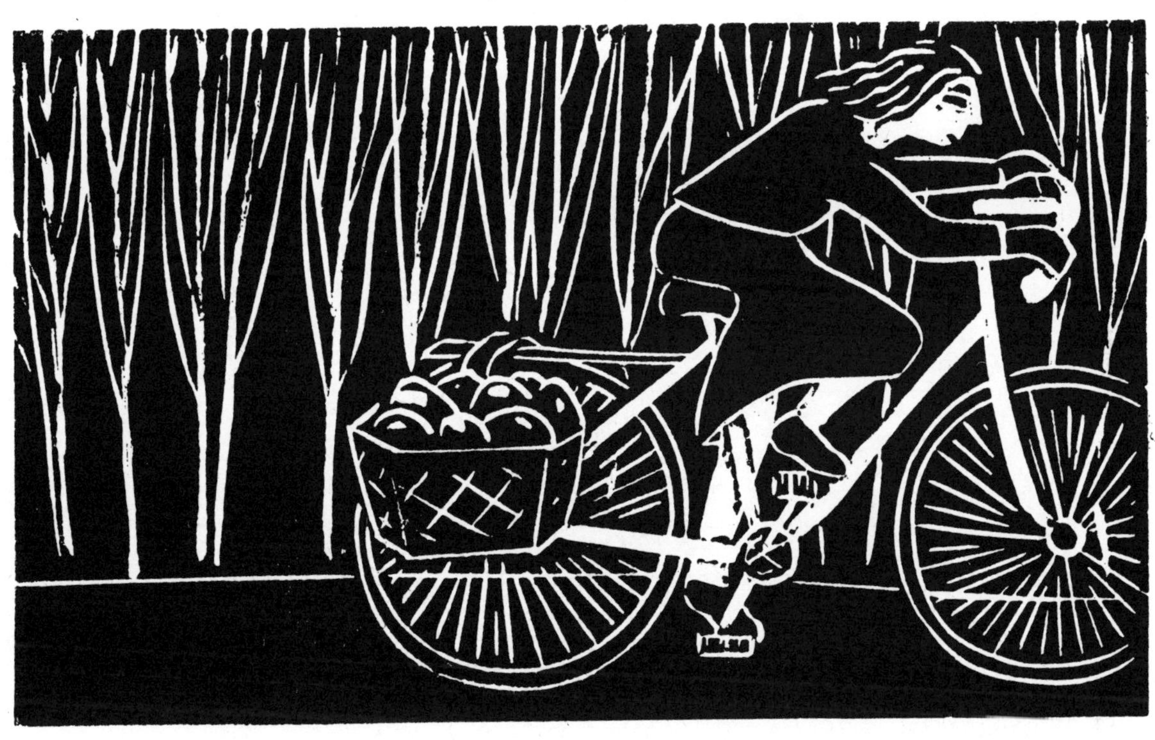

ONCE THE GERMANS STOPPED ME AT A CANAL, DEMANDING MY LOAD OF SUGAR BEETS. I REFUSED. LUCKILY PEOPLE IN A ROWBOAT TOOK ME ABOARD. THE SS SHOT AT US AS WE ROWED OFF, BUT WE ESCAPED.

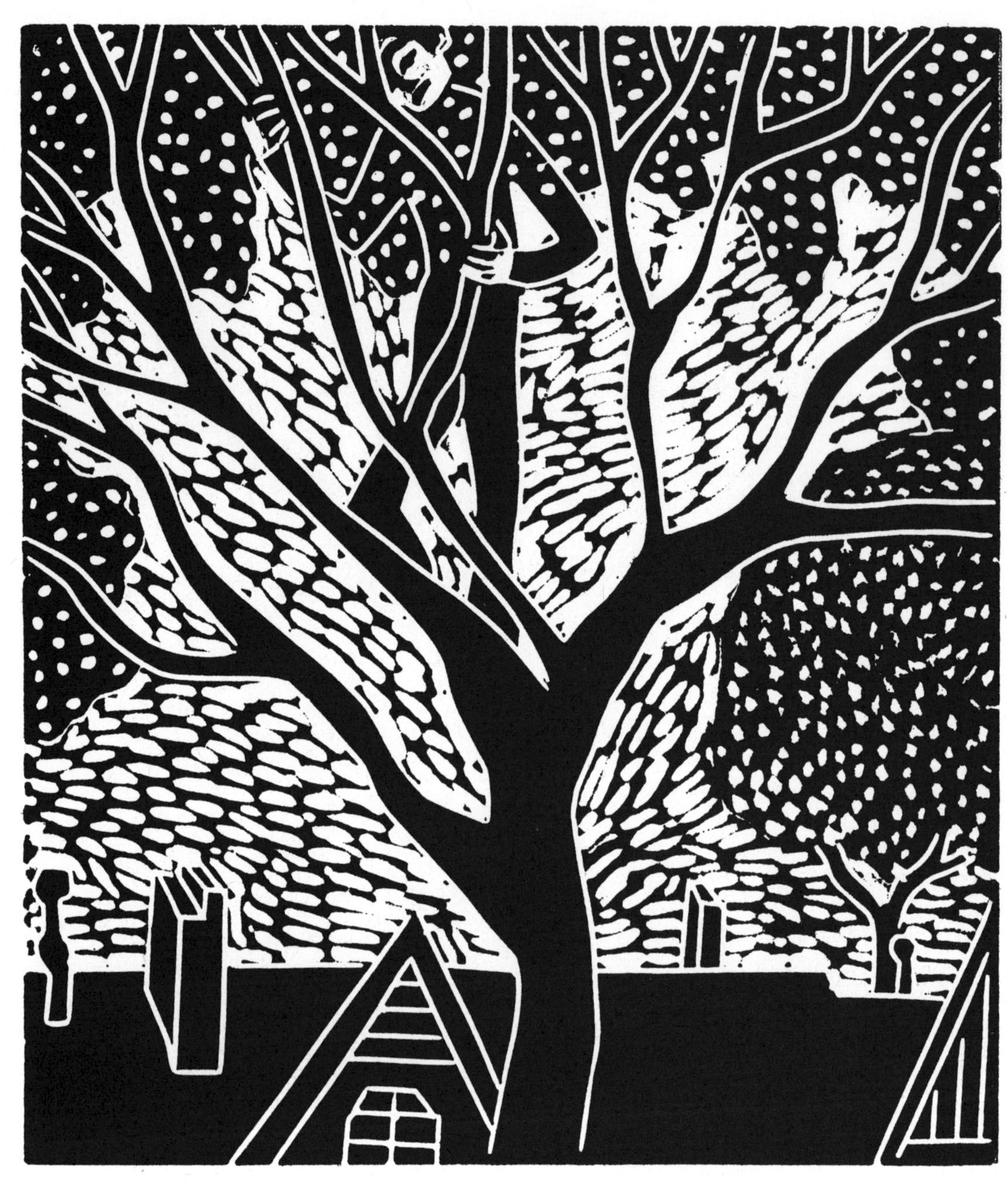

SOMETIMES THE SS CORDONED OFF SEVERAL BLOCKS AND THEN PEOPLE DISAPPEARED. ONCE I WENT OUT WHEN THEY WERE SEARCHING OUR NEIGHBORHOOD. WHEN I LOOKED UP I SAW A MAN HIDING IN THE TOP OF A TREE, BUT THE SS DID NOT SEE HIM.

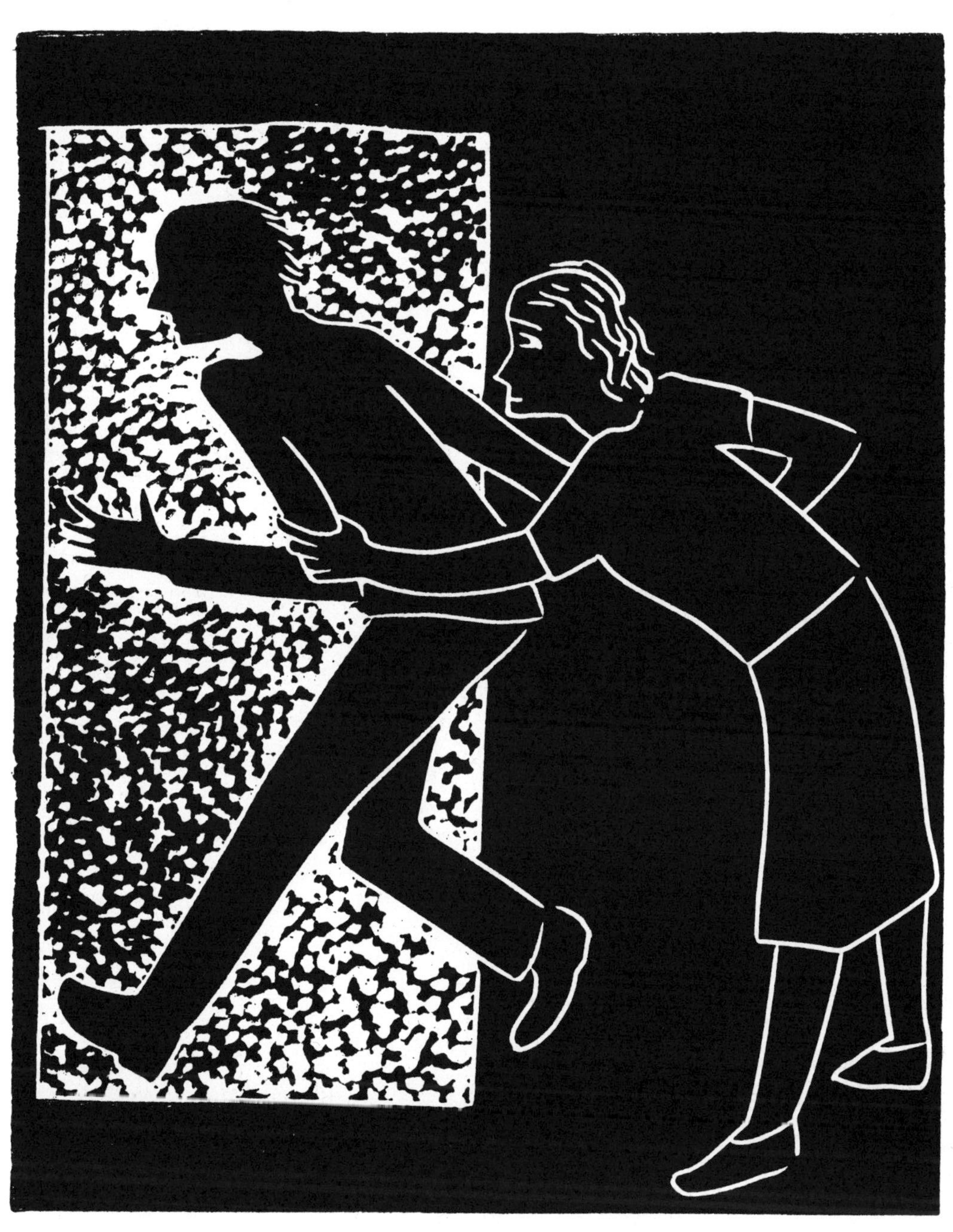

I CAME HOME AND WARNED THE JEWS. TWO HID DOWNSTAIRS, BUT THE THIRD PANICKED AND TRIED TO RUN OUT THE BACK DOOR. I HIT HIM AS HARD AS I COULD AND DRAGGED HIM INSIDE. IF ANYONE HAD SEEN HIM WE WOULD ALL HAVE BEEN IN DANGER.

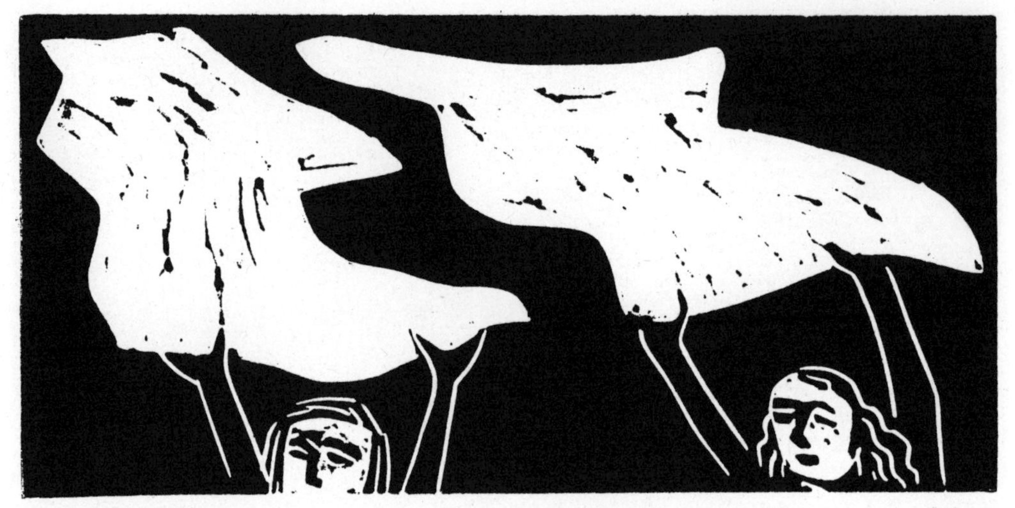

THE SWEDISH RED CROSS AIRLIFTED WHITE BREAD AND CHOCOLATE. THE PACKAGES WERE DROPPED IN A BIG WHITE SQUARE. FROM A NEIGHBOR'S ROOF WE WAVED WHITE SHEETS AT THE PLANES.

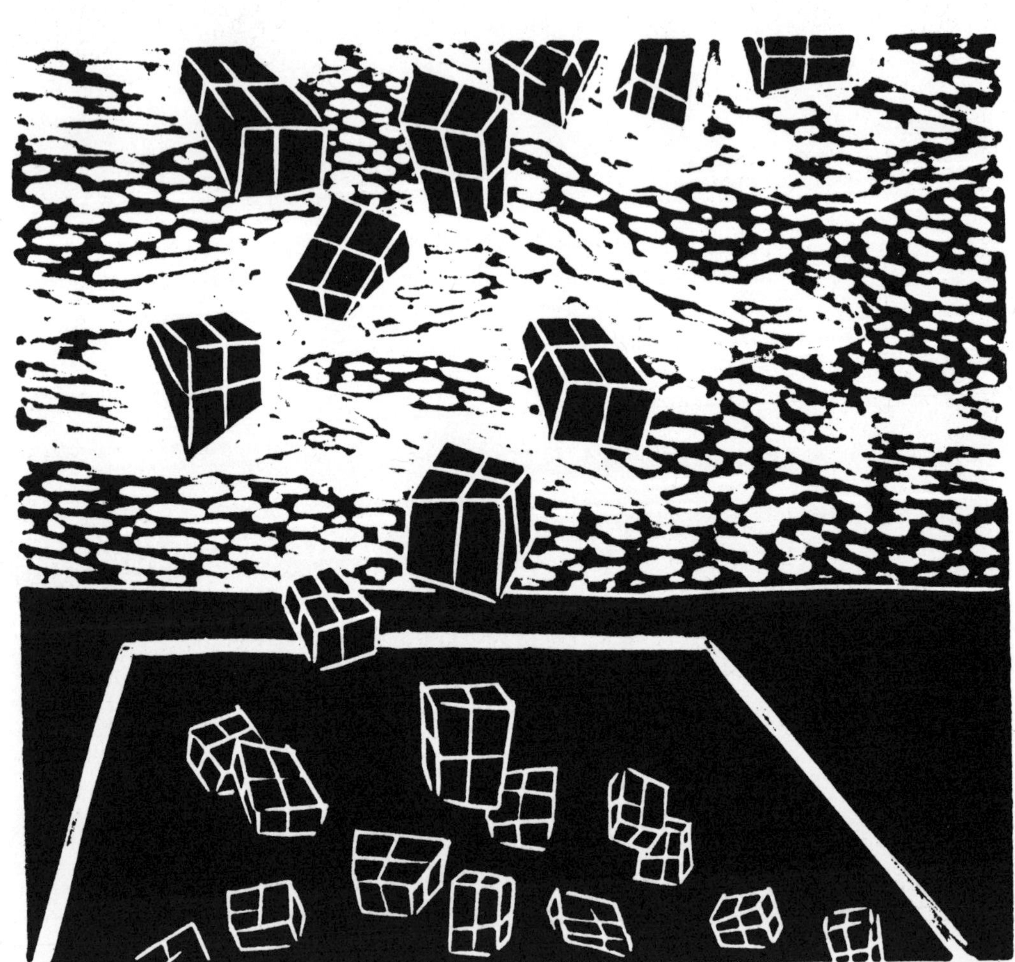

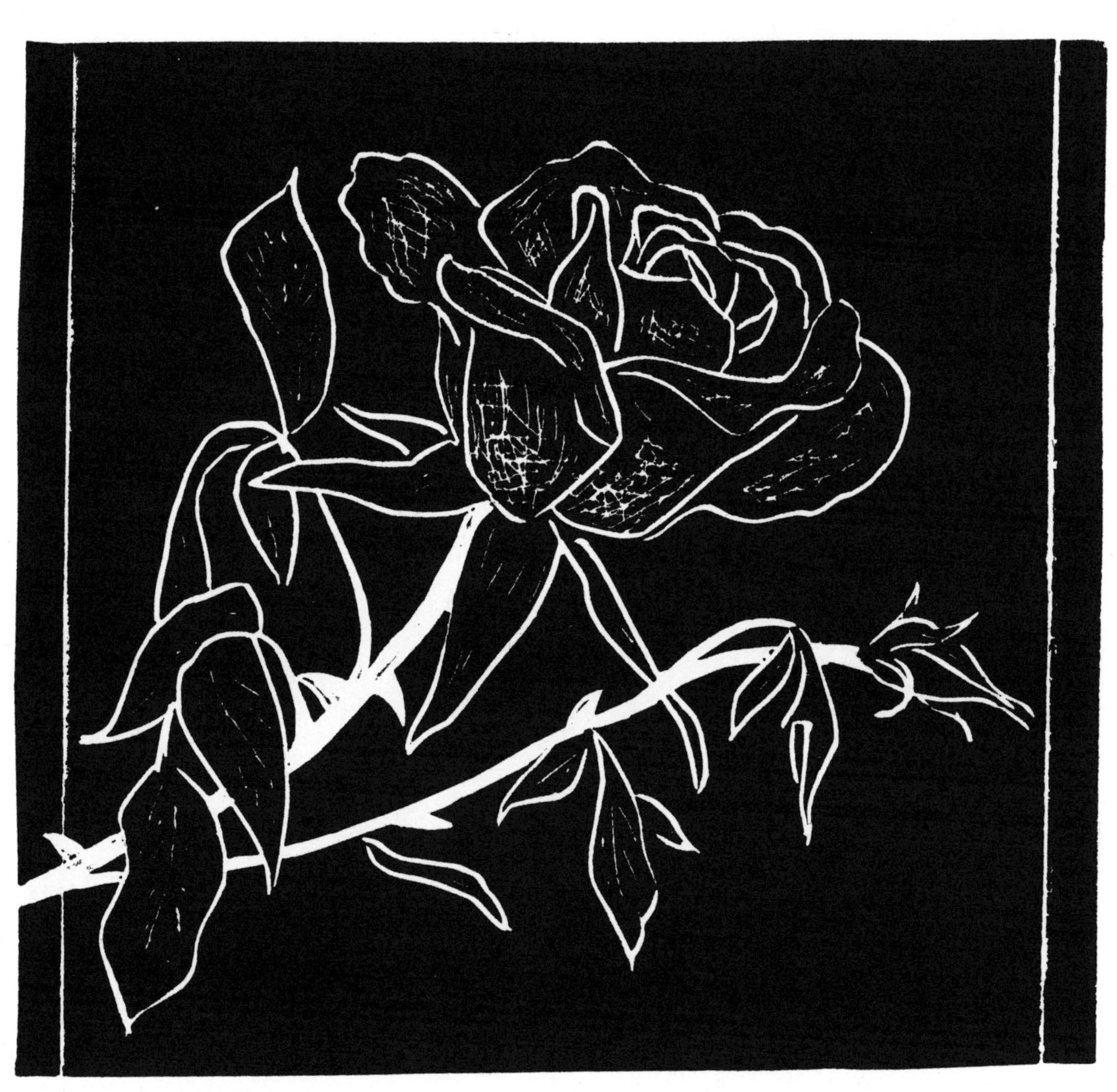

WHEN THE GERMANS KILLED SOMEONE WE PUT FLOWERS ON THE SIDEWALK WHERE THEY DIED. TOWARD THE END OF THE WAR THE KILLINGS INCREASED SO MUCH THAT THE SIDEWALKS WERE ALWAYS FULL OF FLOWERS

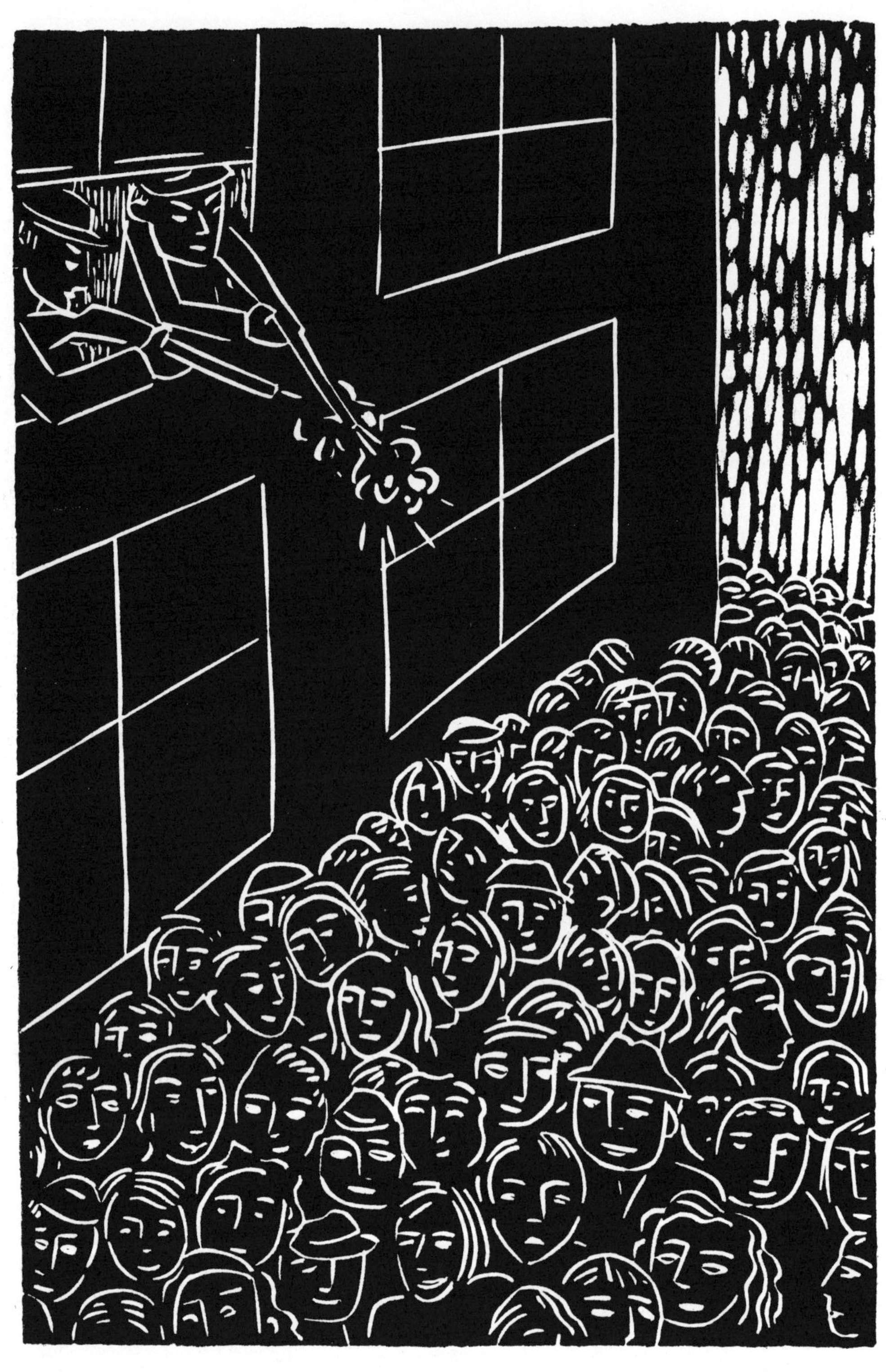

THE DAY THE WAR ENDED PEOPLE WENT TO CELEBRATE IN THE MAIN SQUARE. SOME GESTAPO SHOT INTO THE CROWD FROM A HOTELWINDOW. SO OUR REAL CELEBRATIONS DID NOT START UNTIL THE NEXT DAY.

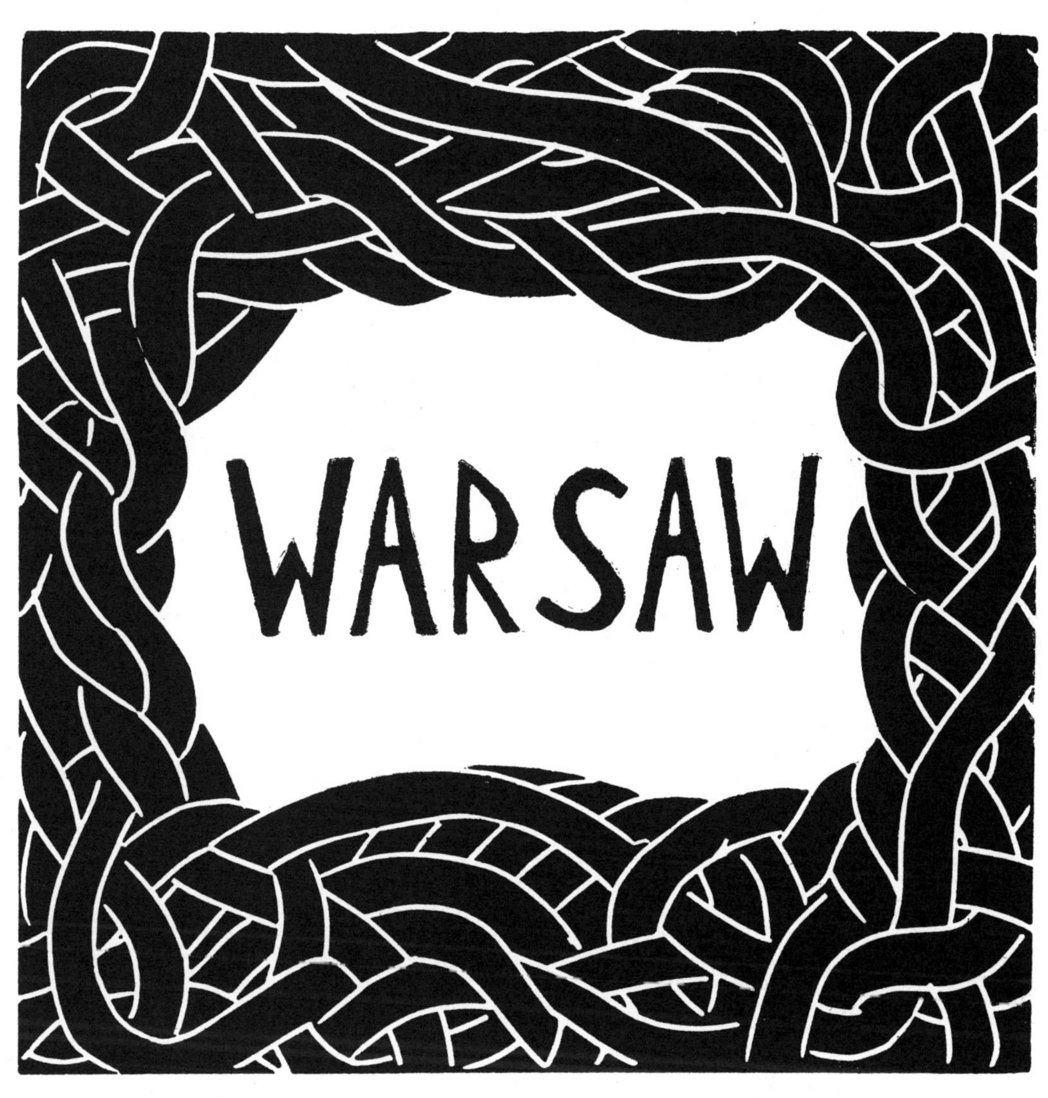
WARSAW

Before the war, there were approximately 3.3 million Jews in Poland, which represented 10% of the total population and was the largest concentration of Jews anywhere in the world. Although both official and unofficial anti-Semitism increased dramatically in Poland in the years immediately preceding the war, Jews remained vital and active participants in Polish economic life and politics. In 1931, there were over 350,000 Jews in Warsaw, about 30% of the city's population.

Hitler invaded Poland on September 1, 1939. However, Warsaw, the country's capital, did not fall until September 27, 1939, and German troops waited for several more days before entering the city. At first, Jews such as **Alexander Groth** and his family continued to live in their prewar homes. They were still there in the spring of 1940 for the celebration of Passover, but it was not long before Polish Jews were segregated from the rest of the population.

The first Polish ghetto was established in Lódz on May 1, 1940. The Warsaw Ghetto, which covered about 400 acres, was established in November 1940 and at its peak had a population of 445,000. This meant that 30% of the city's total population, plus any Jews transported from other cities, was confined to 2.4% of the city's total area. By the middle of 1941, nearly 5,000 Jews a month were dying of illness and starvation.

In 1942, conditions in the Warsaw Ghetto grew progressively worse, culminating in the deportations that began in July of that year. Between July 22 and August 12, 1942, over 250,000 Jews were taken from the ghetto to the death camp at Treblinka, and more were deported in the months that followed. By September 1942, those Jews who had been spared owing to their status as skilled workers were also deported. Realizing that special permits or jobs could no longer save them, Jews such as Alexander Groth and his mother, who had adequate financial resources, went into hiding outside the ghetto. The roundups continued, and by the spring of 1943 only about 60,000 Jews remained in the ghetto. On April 19, the Jewish Fighting Organization of the Warsaw Ghetto staged an armed revolt against the Nazis. The fighting lasted for weeks, until the Germans finally burned the ghetto to the ground.

As the Soviet army advanced towards Warsaw in August 1944, the Polish underground rose up against the Nazi regime. However, the Soviet troops halted just outside Warsaw, giving the Germans time to crush the Polish resistance and deport the survivors, many to Auschwitz.

The last German troops were not driven out of Poland by the Soviets until early in 1945. By that time, only about 250,000 Jews remained alive. Three million, over 90% of the Polish Jewish population, had been murdered.

After the war, Alexander Groth and his mother returned to Warsaw to look for relatives. They found the body of his stepfather, whom they buried in a Jewish cemetery, but all of their other Polish relatives were gone. In 1946, they went to Sweden, and from there, in March 1947, they immigrated to the United States.

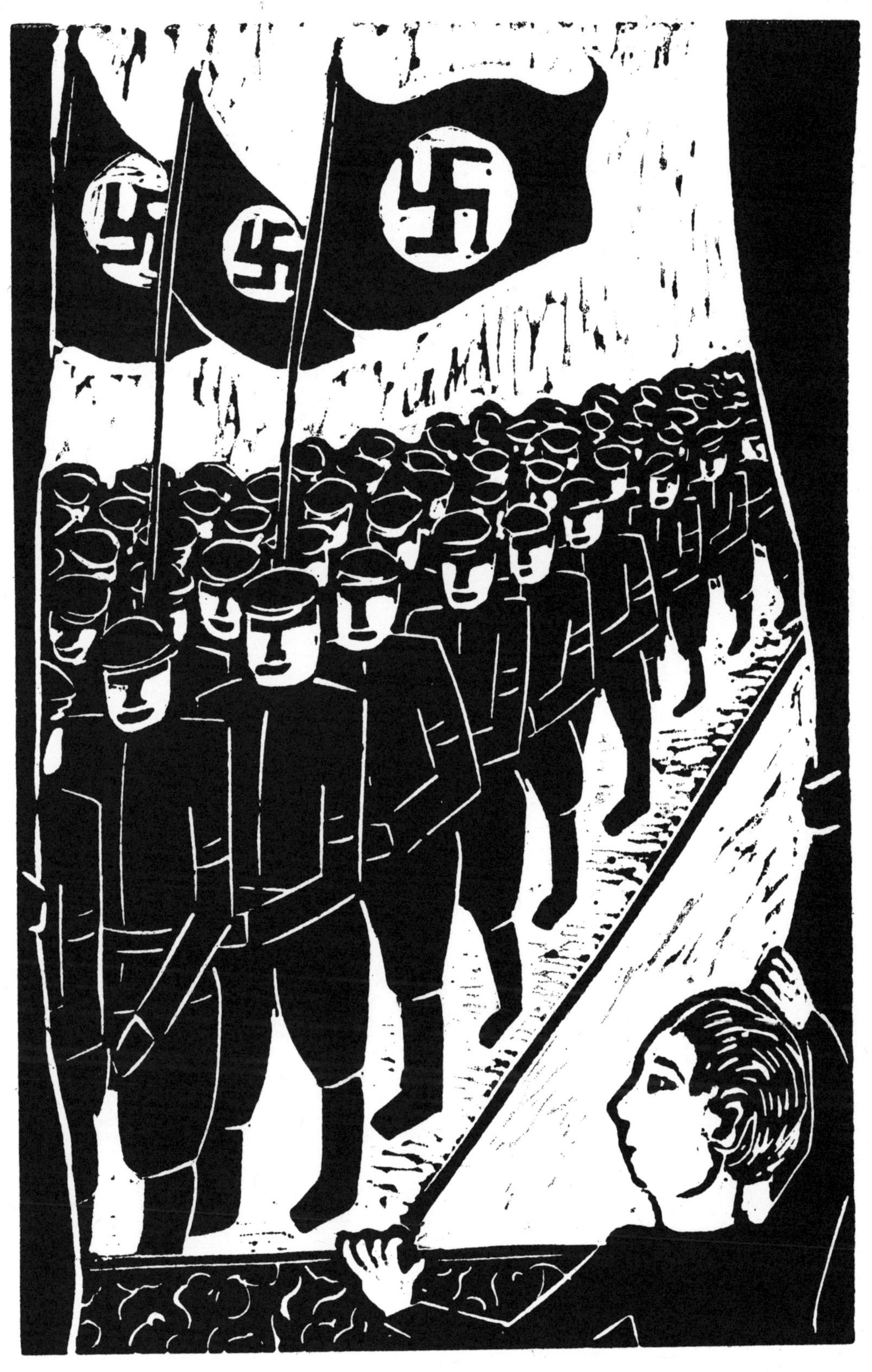

OCTOBER 5, 1939. FROM OUR WINDOW I WATCHED THE VICTORIOUS NAZI TROOPS PARADE THROUGH WARSAW. THE GERMANS LOOKED INVINCIBLE.

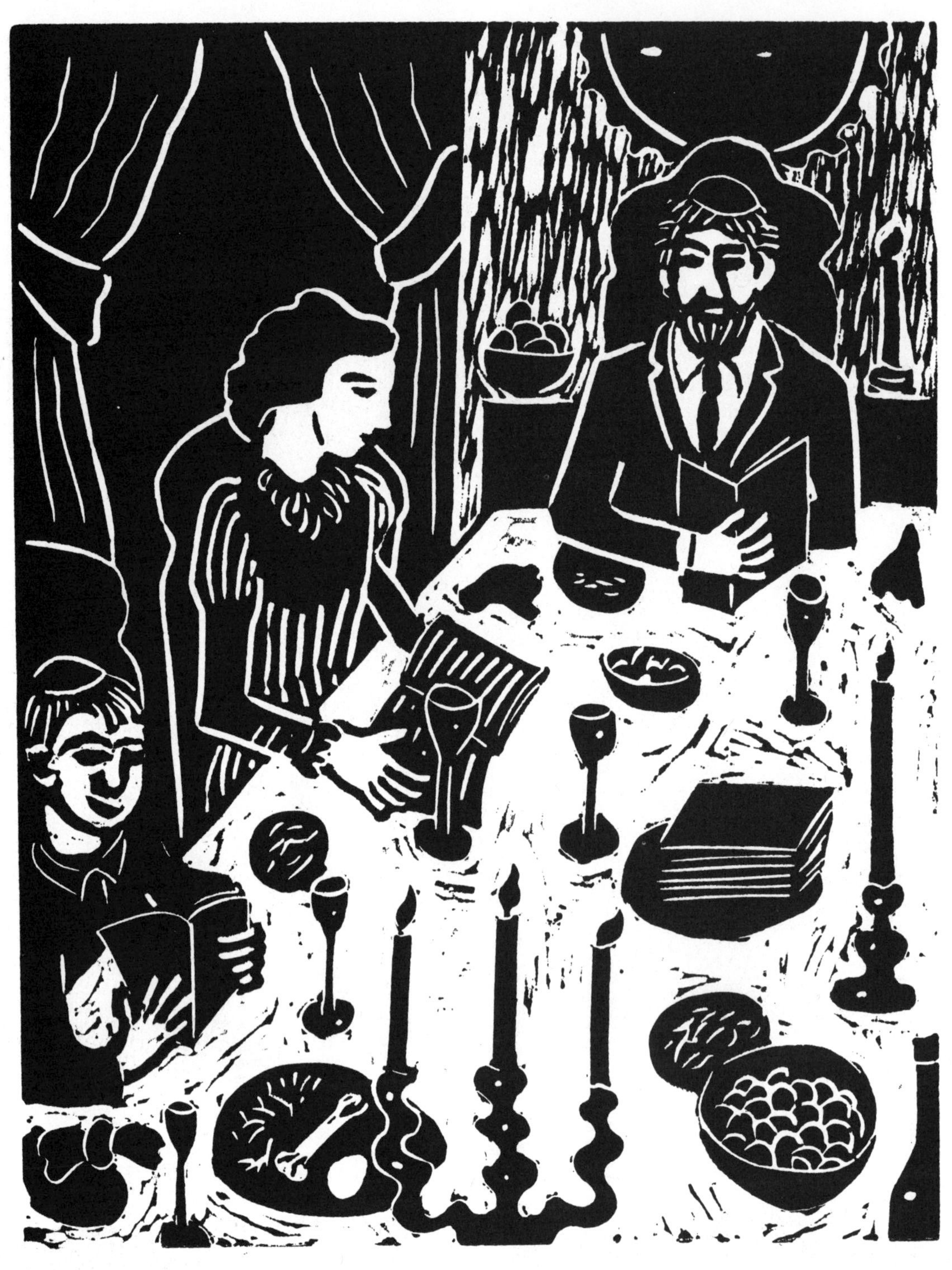

MY PARENTS WERE ASSIMILATED JEWS WHO CULTIVATED NON-JEWISH APPEARANCE AND SPEECH. AT HOME WE SPOKE POLISH, NOT YIDDISH. IN 1940, WHEN I WAS SEVEN, WE CELEBRATED PASSOVER AT MY GRANDPARENTS'. IT WAS OUR LAST SEDER IN POLAND.

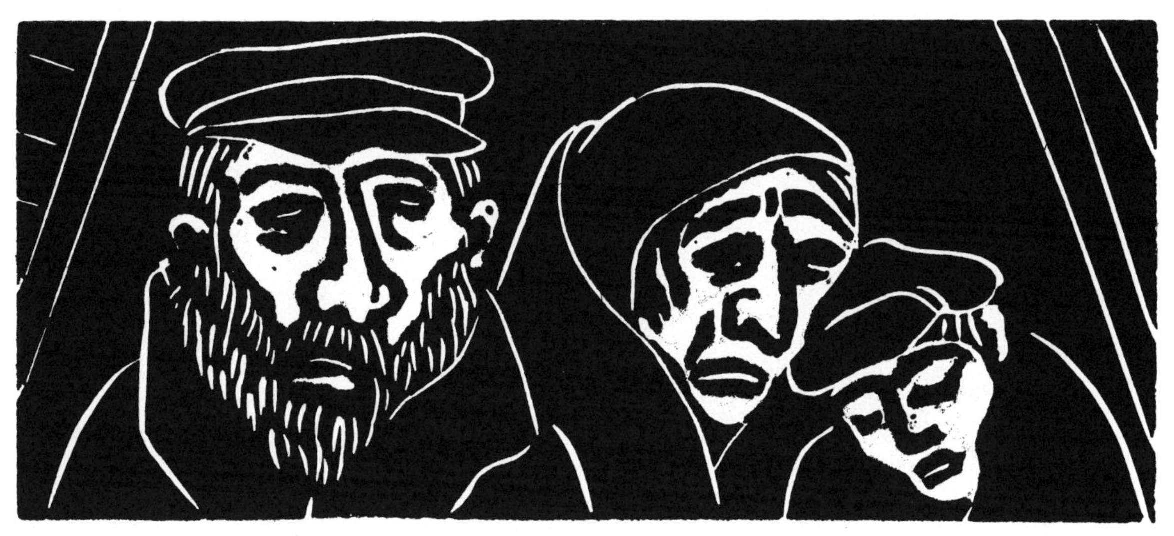

IN 1940 WE WERE FORCED TO MOVE TO THE WARSAW GHETTO. BECAUSE MY STEPFATHER HAD SAVED A LOT OF MONEY WE HAD ENOUGH FOOD AND WARM CLOTHES. WE EVEN HAD OUR OWN APARTMENT. BUT EVERYWHERE OUTSIDE I SAW PEOPLE STARVING AND FREEZING. HUNGER AND DISEASE KILLED THOUSANDS. DEAD BODIES WERE LEFT LYING IN THE STREET.

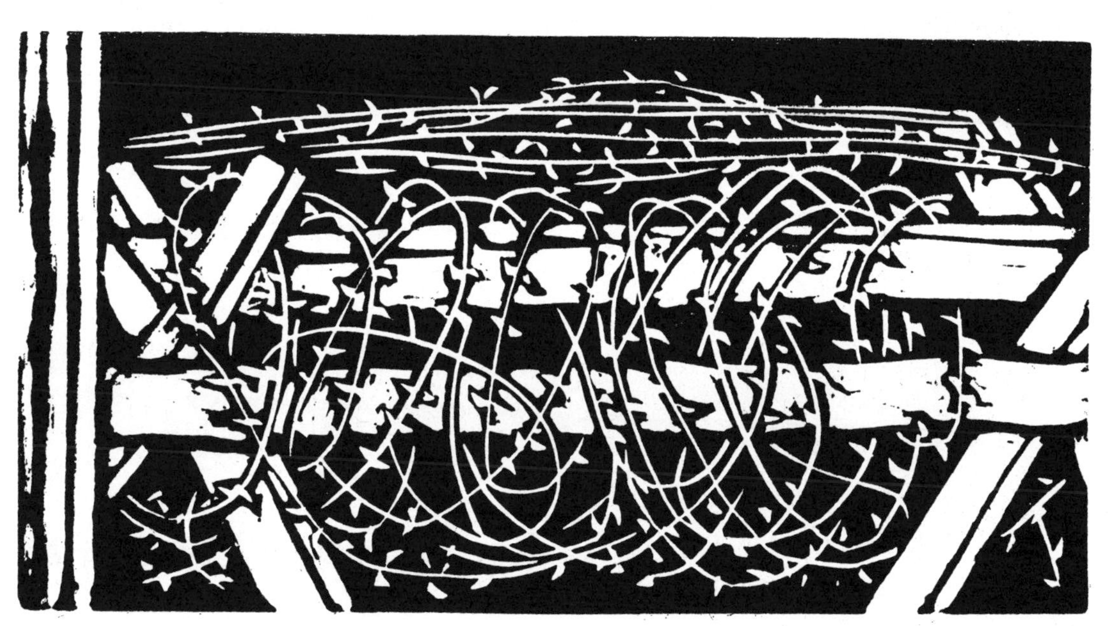

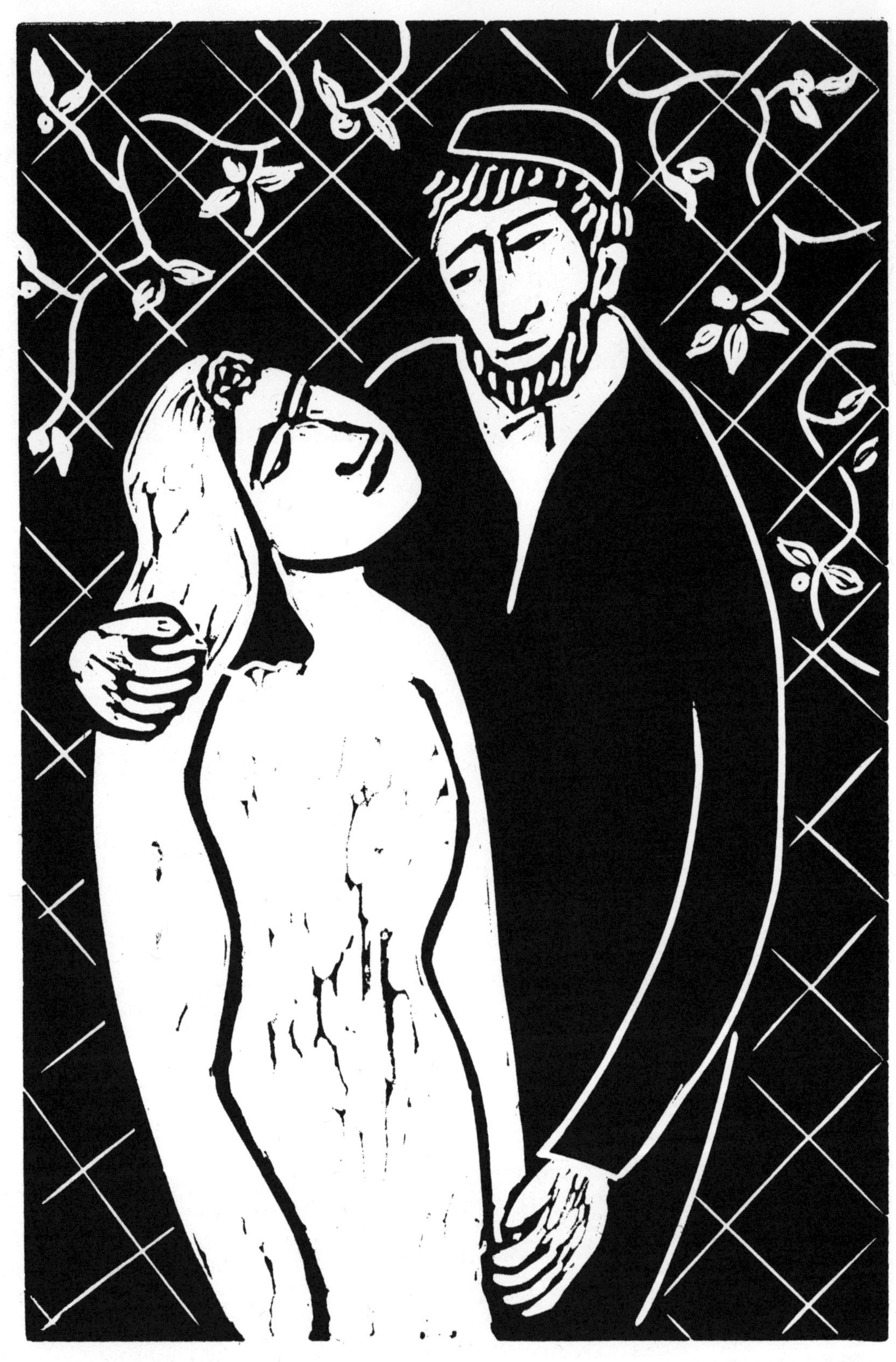

IN 1942 THERE WAS A WEDDING IN OUR BUILDING. IT WAS VERY HAPPY AND FESTIVE. I THOUGHT "DON'T THEY KNOW WHAT IS HAPPENING?"

THAT SUMMER, MASS DEPORTATIONS BEGAN FROM THE GHETTO. JEWS LIKE MY BLIND GRANDMOTHER, WHO WERE NOT FIT FOR TRANSPORT, WERE SIMPLY EXECUTED. MY GRANDFATHER REFUSED TO LET HER GO ALONE, SO THEY WERE BOTH TAKEN TO THE JEWISH CEMETERY AND SHOT BY THE NAZI SOLDIERS.

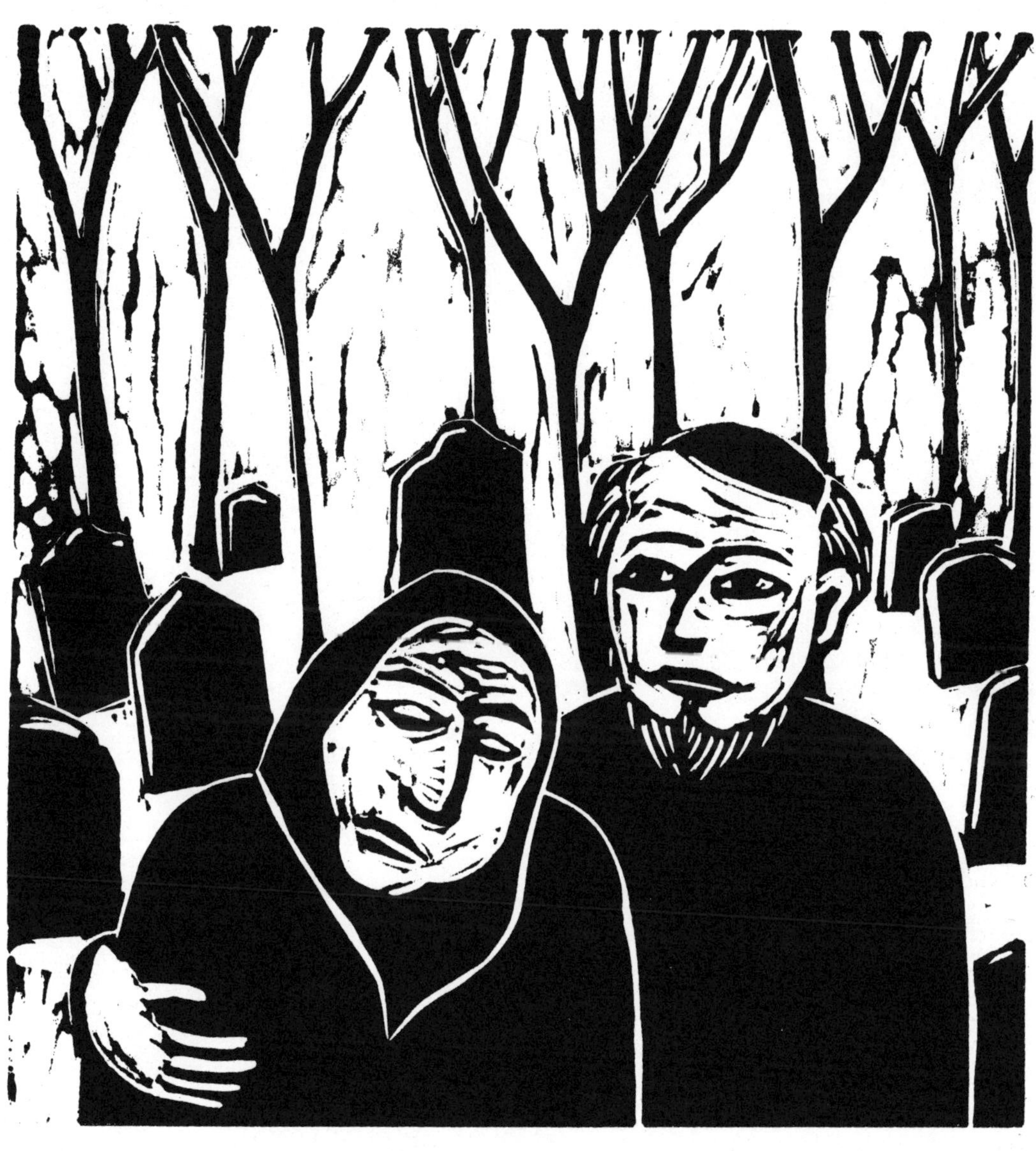

FINALLY I UNDERSTOOD IT WOULD TAKE A MIRACLE FOR US TO SURVIVE

MY MOTHER GOT A JOB IN A FACTORY OUTSIDE THE GHETTO. ALTHOUGH IT WAS ILLEGAL FOR ME TO GO WITH HER, SHE TOOK ME AND HID ME IN A BOX OF SOCKS.

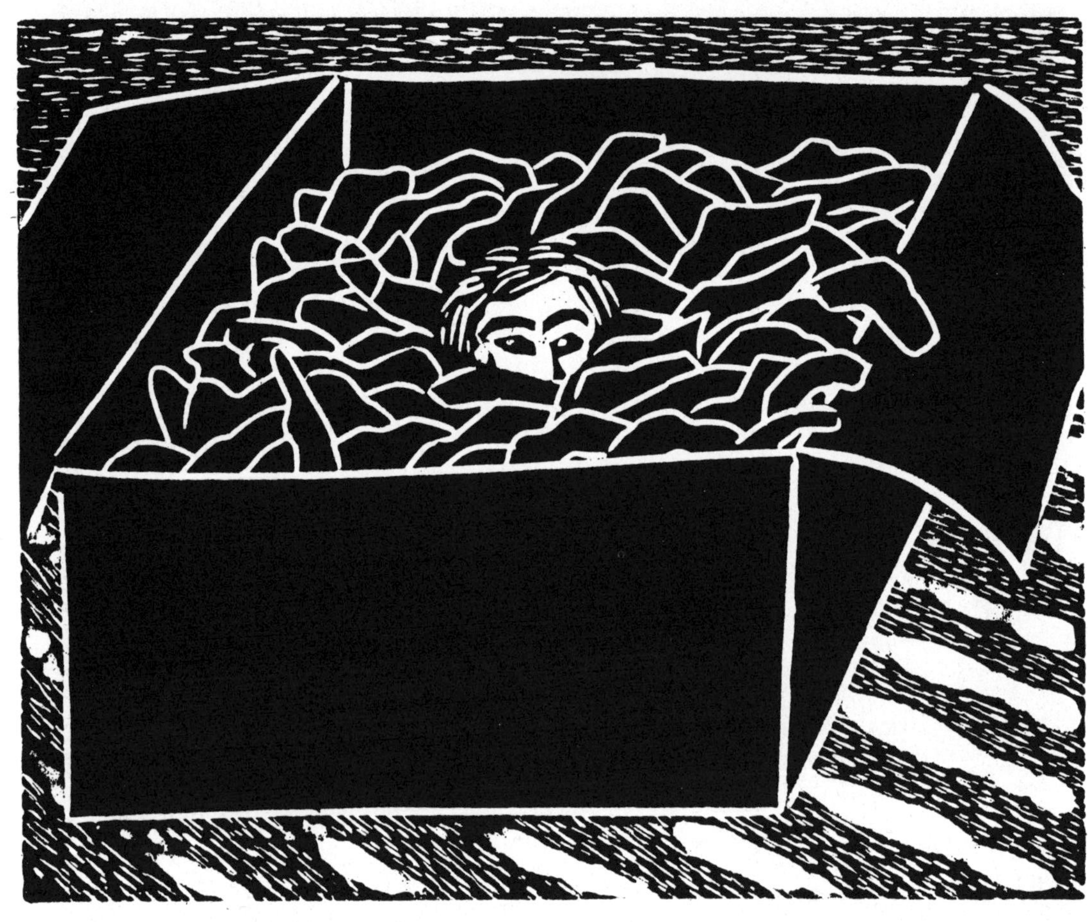

ONE DAY I HEARD GUNSHOTS AND SHOUTS OF "RAUS". IT WAS A SELECTION TO DEPORT ANY JEWS WHO WERE NOT SUPPOSED TO BE IN THE FACTORY. MY MOTHER AND I GOT IN LINE IN THE COURTYARD BEFORE THE SS WITH THEIR WHIPS, DOGS AND MACHINE GUNS. OUR TURN CAME, THE SS LOOKED AT MY MOTHER'S PAPERS AND LET US BOTH GO.

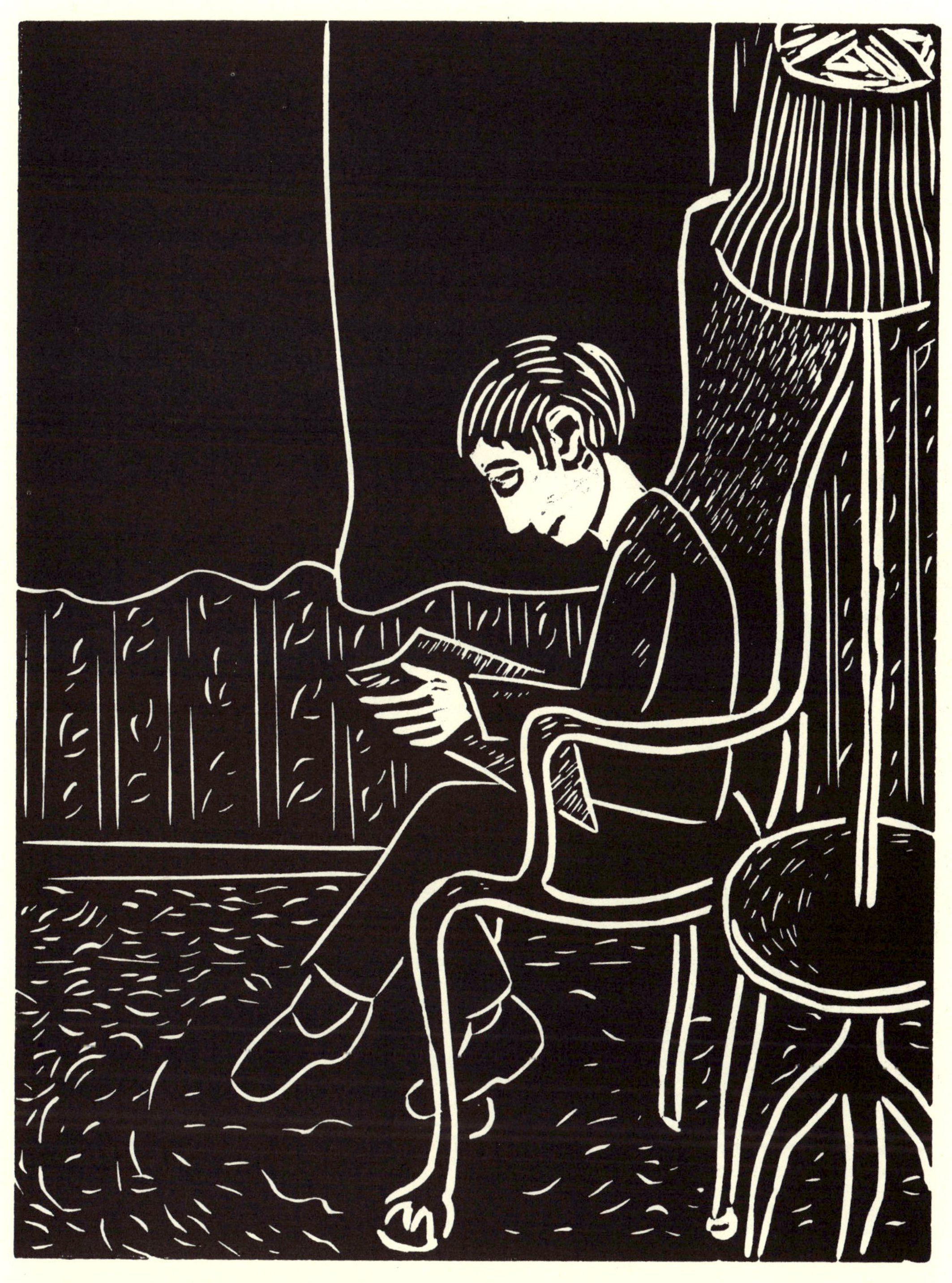

SUMMER, 1942. MY MOTHER TOOK ME OUT OF THE GHETTO TO THE HOME OF POLISH FRIENDS. FOR TWO YEARS I NEVER JUMPED OR RAN OR LOOKED OUT A WINDOW. I ALWAYS HAD TO BE VERY QUIET. I NEVER SAW ANOTHER CHILD. I READ POLISH NEWSPAPERS. AND I COULD NEVER GO OUTSIDE.

THE NAZIS WERE ALWAYS LOOKING FOR JEWS IN WARSAW. THEY GAVE REWARDS OF MONEY AND OF FOOD TO ANYONE WHO TURNED IN JEWS. ALTHOUGH WE HAD FALSE POLISH PAPERS, WE WERE IN DANGER.

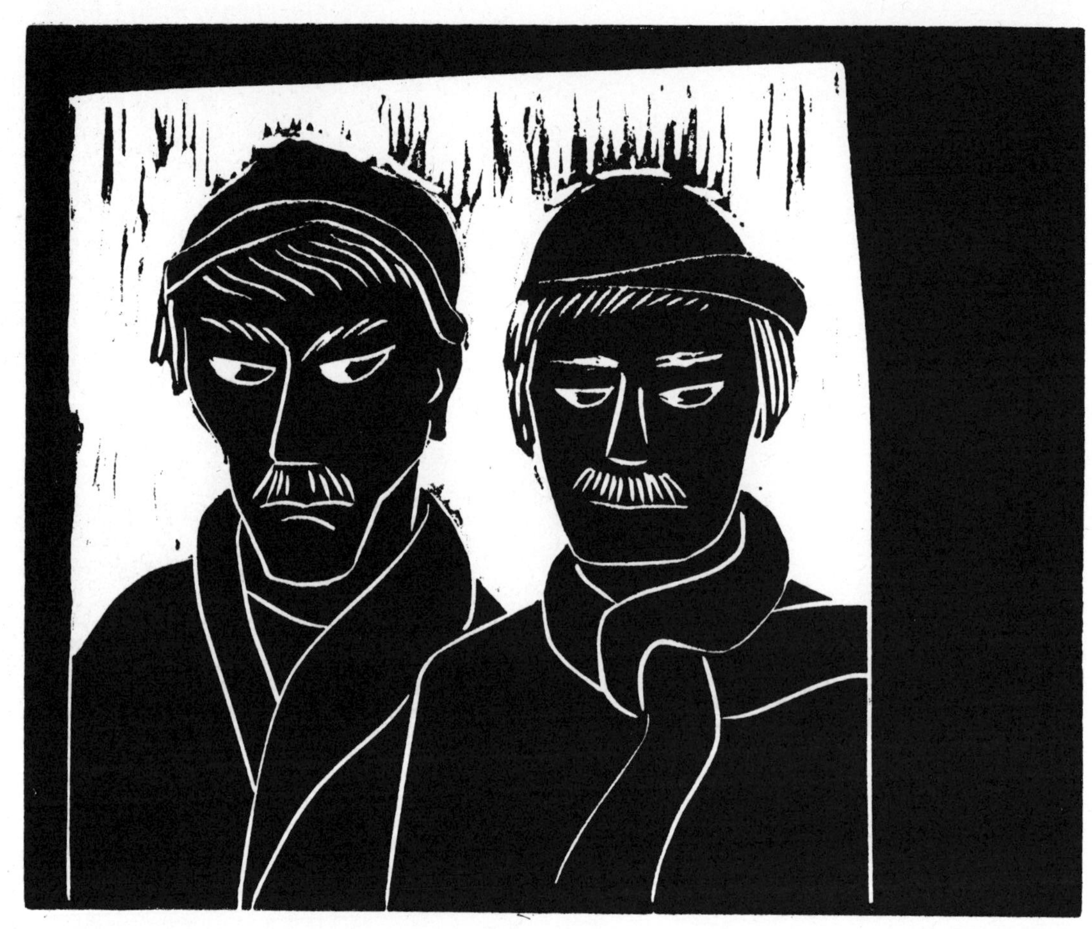

ONE DAY WHEN WE WERE ALONE TWO STRANGE MEN CAME AND DEMANDED MONEY. MOTHER GAVE THEM SOME GOLD COINS. AFTER THAT, WE TRIED TO FIND ANOTHER PLACE TO LIVE BUT THERE WAS NO PLACE WE COULD GO. LUCKILY THE BLACKMAILERS NEVER RETURNED

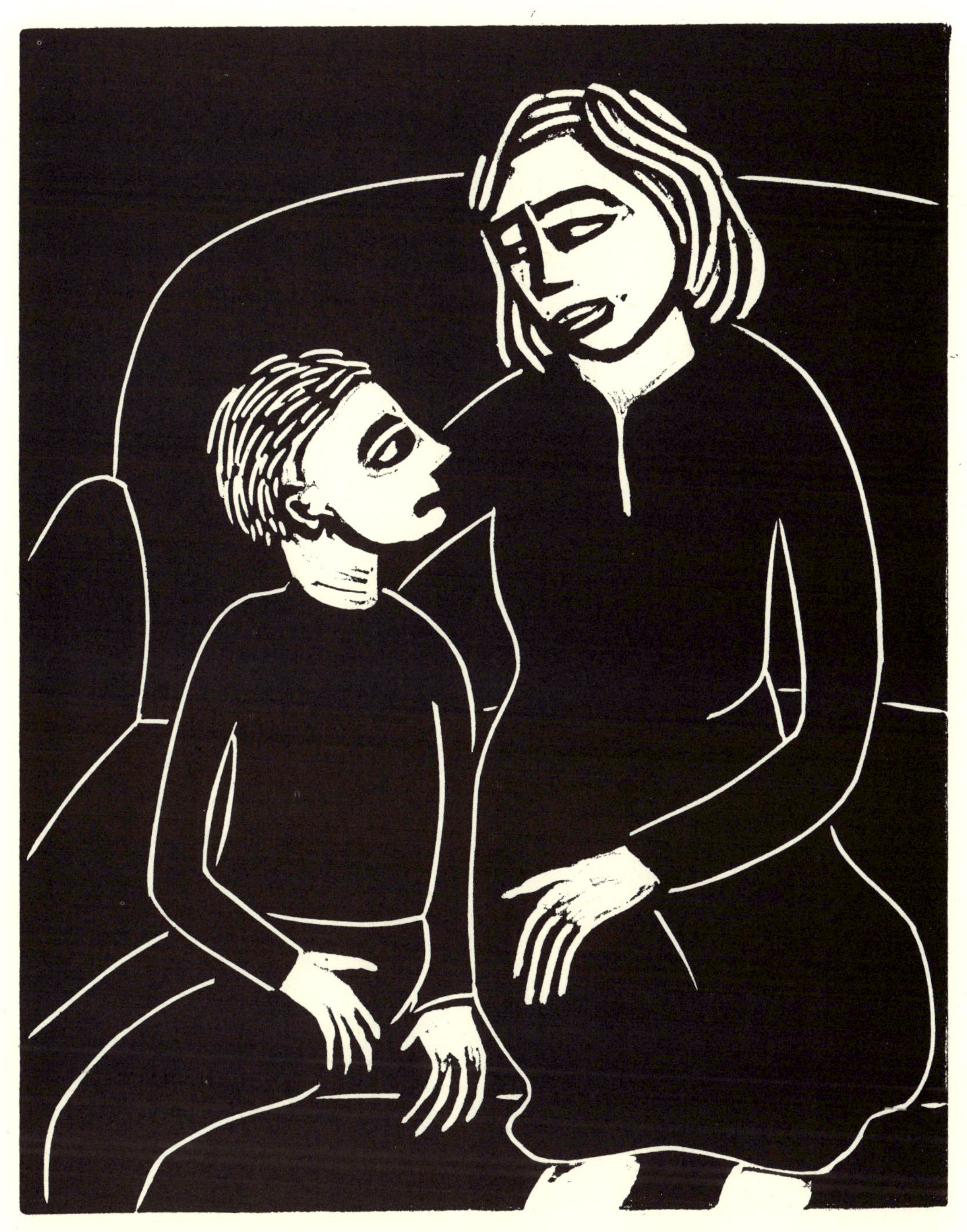

MY MOTHER TOLD STORIES AND WE PLAYED GAMES. SHE ALWAYS CALLED ME JANUSZ, A FALSE POLISH NAME, AND WE SPOKE POLISH, SO IF WE WERE DISCOVERED, I COULD PRETEND TO BE A POLE. SHE HAD SOME CYANIDE PILLS. I KNEW WE COULD TAKE THEM IF NECESSARY.

SUMMER, 1944. AS THE RUSSIAN ARMY ADVANCED, POLISH RESISTANCE INCREASED. FINALLY THE NAZIS BOMBED WARSAW. WHEN THE POLES GAVE UP, HITLER ORDERED THE EVACUATION OF WARSAW. ALONG WITH OUR FRIENDS, WE WERE LOADED INTO A CATTLE CAR.

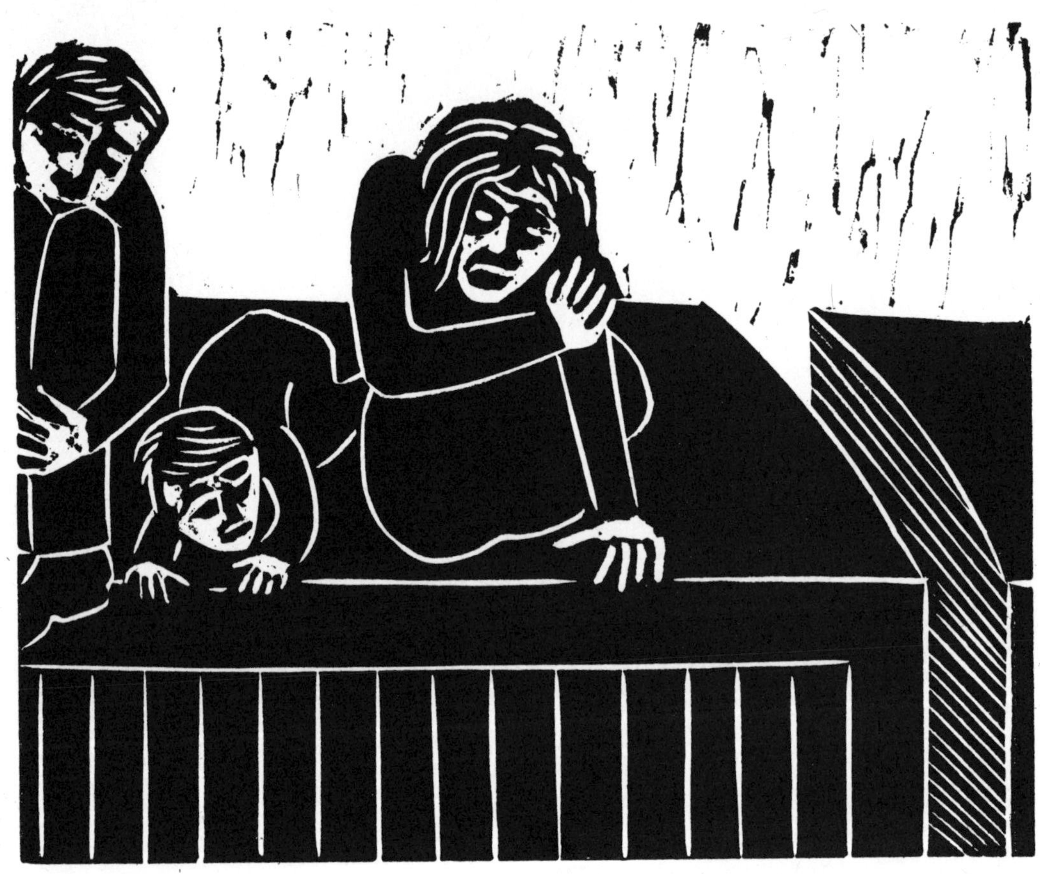

A POLISH RAILROAD WORKER TOLD US THAT OUR TRAIN WAS HEADED TO AUSCHWITZ. AT THE NEXT STOP WE CLIMBED ON THE ROOF. WHEN THE SS WAS NOT LOOKING, WE JUMPED OFF THE TRAIN AND HID IN THE BUSHES. WE WERE ONLY ONE STOP FROM AUSCHWITZ.

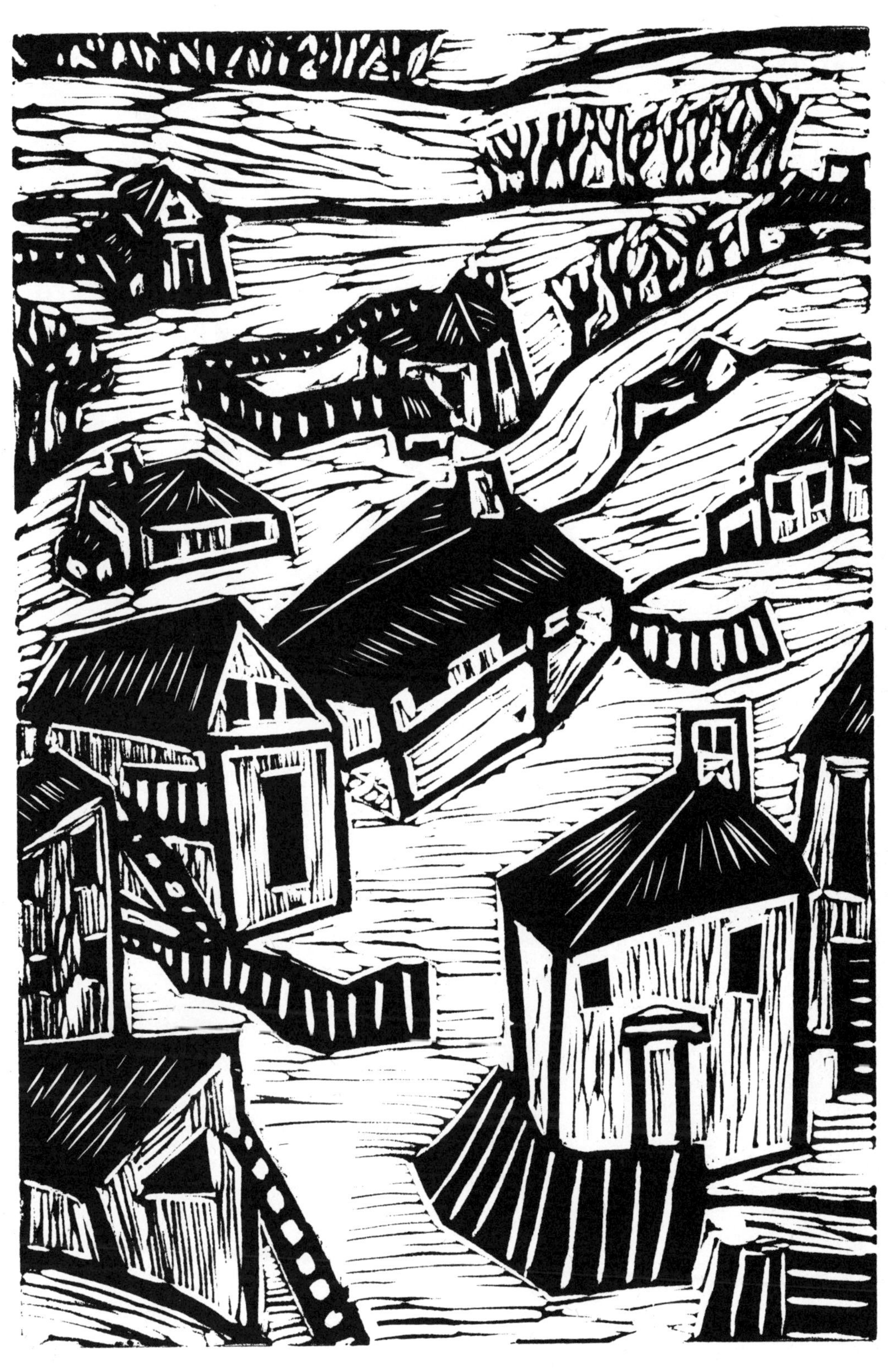

AT A NEARBY HOUSE WE WERE FED BY A POLISH FARMER. HE TOLD US THE WAY TO CRACOW. IN A VILLAGE NEAR CRACOW OUR FRIENDS' RELATIVES AGREED TO HIDE US FROM THE NAZIS.

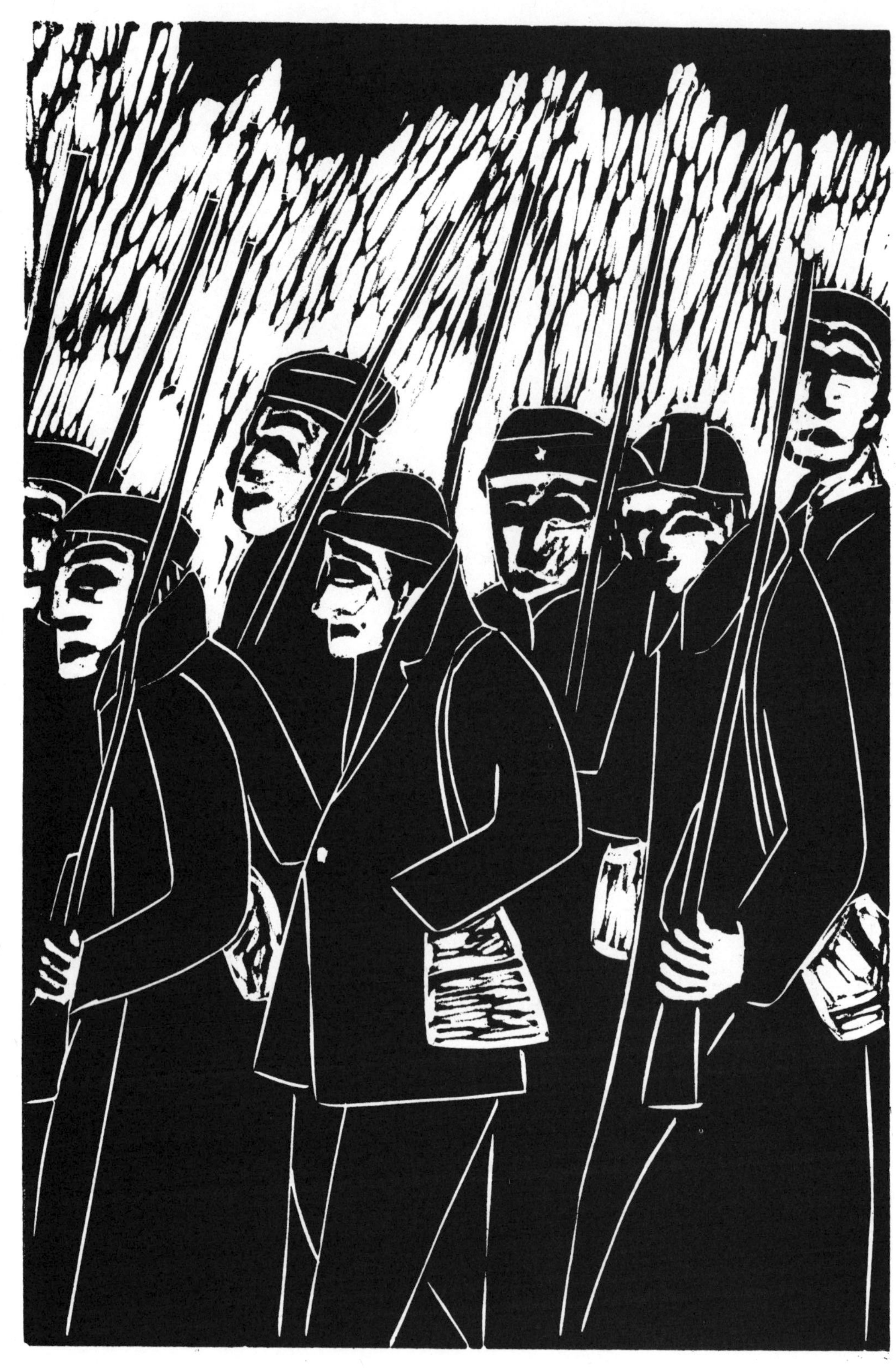

JANUARY, 1945. RUSSIAN SOLDIERS, LOOKING RAGGED AND COLD, ARRIVED. I COULD HARDLY BELIEVE THAT THEY HAD DEFEATED THE GERMAN ARMY.

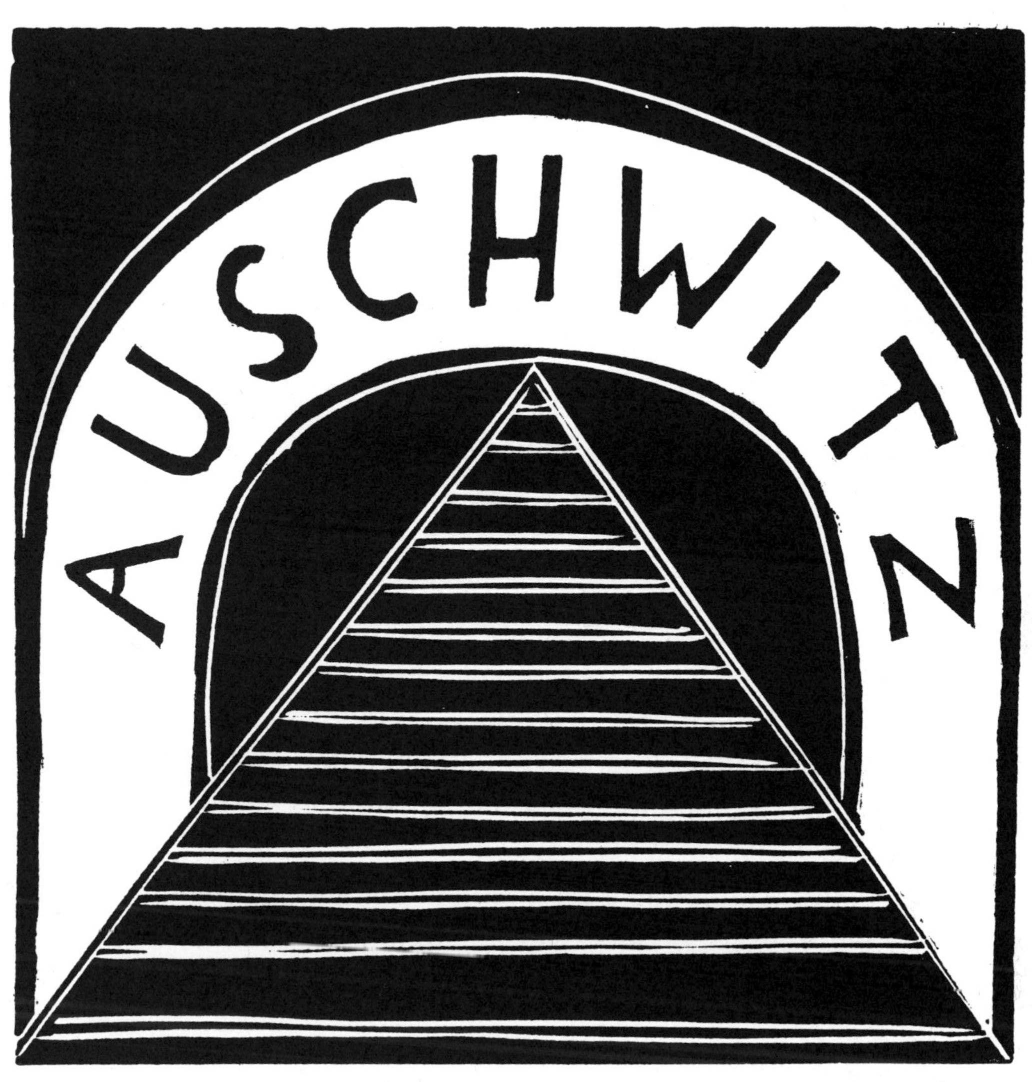
AUSCHWITZ

Although violent anti-Semitism in Hungary increased dramatically after World War I, Hungarian Jews were relatively secure in the years immediately preceding World War II. In 1938, Hungary had allied itself with Germany, and in return it was permitted to annex parts of Czechoslovakia and Yugoslavia. These annexations increased the Jewish population in Hungary from 400,000 to over 750,000. Although anti-Jewish laws similar to those in Germany and German-occupied countries were enacted in Hungary starting in 1938, Hungary resisted yellow badges and deportation of Jews until March 19, 1944, when German troops occupied the country.

The Nazis began deporting Hungarian Jews in the spring of 1944, and shortly thereafter between 12,000 and 14,000 Hungarian Jews were being sent to Auschwitz each day. A total of over 450,000 Hungarian Jews (over 70%) were deported, almost all to Auschwitz.

Upon arrival at Auschwitz, Jews were divided into two groups. The elderly and infirm were sent directly to the gas chambers. The young and healthy were sent to the forced labor section of the camp, where their heads were shaved and identification numbers tattooed on their arms. **Gloria Lyon**, her mother, and sister got one of the preferred work assignments: "Canada," where the belongings of the deportees were sorted for shipment back to Germany. Those fortunate enough to be assigned to "Canada" had access to food and clothing, which helped them to survive the horrors of the camp.

Josef Mengele, the chief doctor at Auschwitz, conducted medical experiments on Jewish and gypsy twins. Subjects who survived the experiments were summarily put to death. Because Jewish inmates who went to the camp's hospital for illness, injury, or pregnancy were usually sent to the gas chambers, medically trained fellow-inmates often performed secret operations in the barracks. Nazi doctors, including Dr. Mengele, also conducted daily "selections," during which naked inmates were lined up for inspection. Inmates like Gloria, who looked too sick, too weak, or too thin to work, were sent to the gas chambers.

As the war was ending, the Germans tried to blow up the death camps in an attempt to destroy evidence of their crimes against humanity. Surviving inmates were taken in the direction of Germany by train, or they embarked on long "death marches" during which most of the inmates died. In April 1945, Hitler's SS Chief Heinrich Himmler agreed to allow the Swedish Red Cross to transport by train to Sweden 14,000 women who had been released from the camps. Gloria Lyon was one of those women. Other surviving family members returned to Hungary.

When Gloria had an opportunity to immigrate to the United States, the Iron Curtain had already fallen. Unable to bring her family, she came alone to the United States. By the time travel in and out of Hungary was permitted, Gloria's mother had died. She never saw her mother again after Auschwitz.

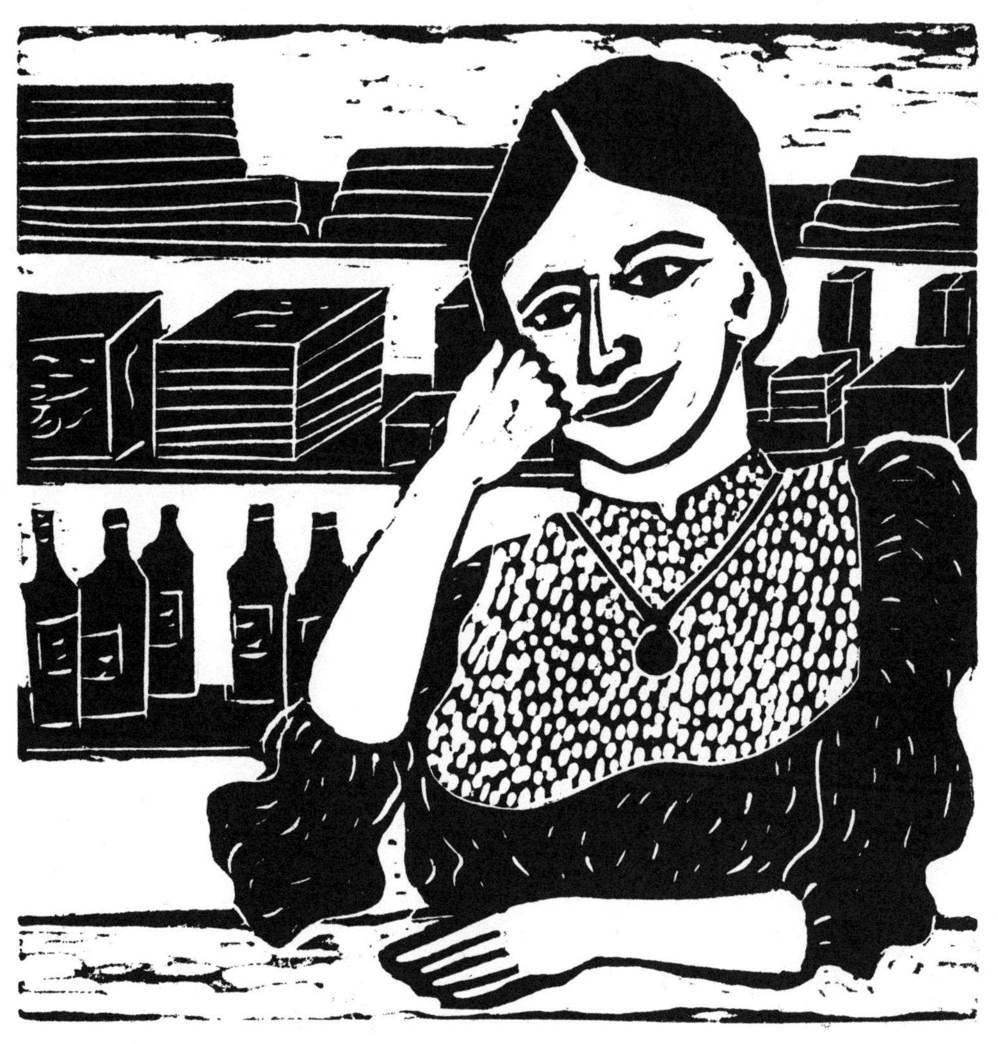

NAGYBEREG, HUNGARY. WE HAD A LARGE FARM WITH VINEYARDS, ORCHARDS AND ANIMALS. MY MOTHER RAN A SMALL VILLAGE STORE. MY FATHER, A LEADER OF THE JEWISH COMMUNITY, WORKED HARMONIOUSLY WITH OUR CHRISTIAN NEIGHBORS.

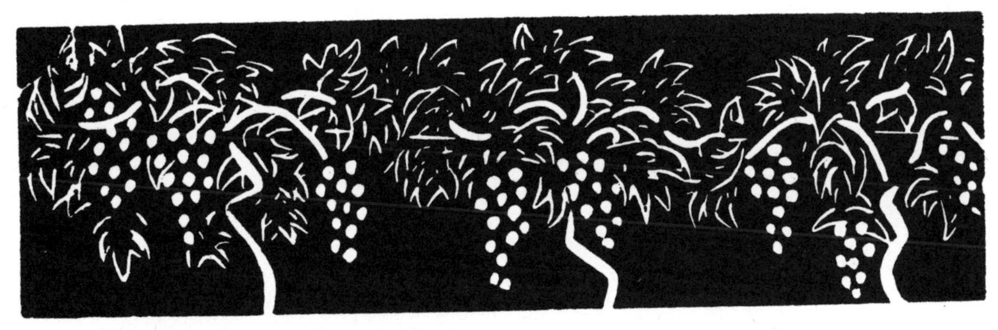

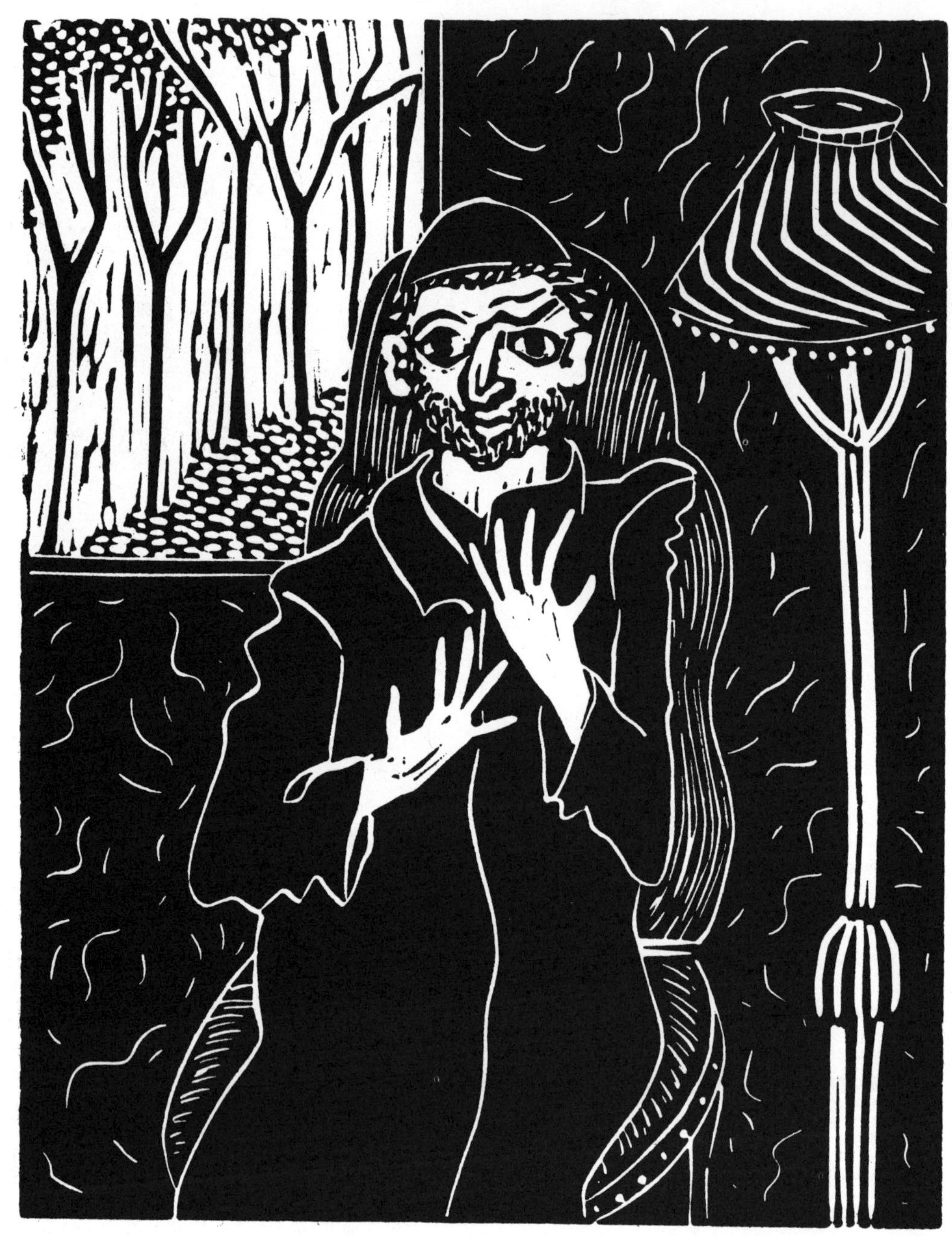

SUMMER, 1943. I WAS 13 YEARS OLD. ONE DAY A STRANGE JEW CAME. HE SAID THAT IN POLAND JEWS WERE FORCED TO DIG THEIR OWN GRAVES. THEN THEY WERE SHOT BY THE NAZIS. HE ESCAPED FROM A MASS GRAVE. BUT NO ONE BELIEVED HIM. MY FATHER TOLD ME NOT TO WORRY, SUCH THINGS COULD NOT HAPPEN IN THE MIDDLE OF THE 20TH CENTURY.

PASSOVER, 1944. A CHRISTIAN FRIEND WARNED US THE GERMANS WOULD COME THE NEXT DAY. MY FATHER CALLED US TOGETHER, AND WE HID OUR SILVER AND JEWELRY UNDER THE FLOOR SO WE COULD FIND THEM WHEN WE RETURNED TO OUR HOME.

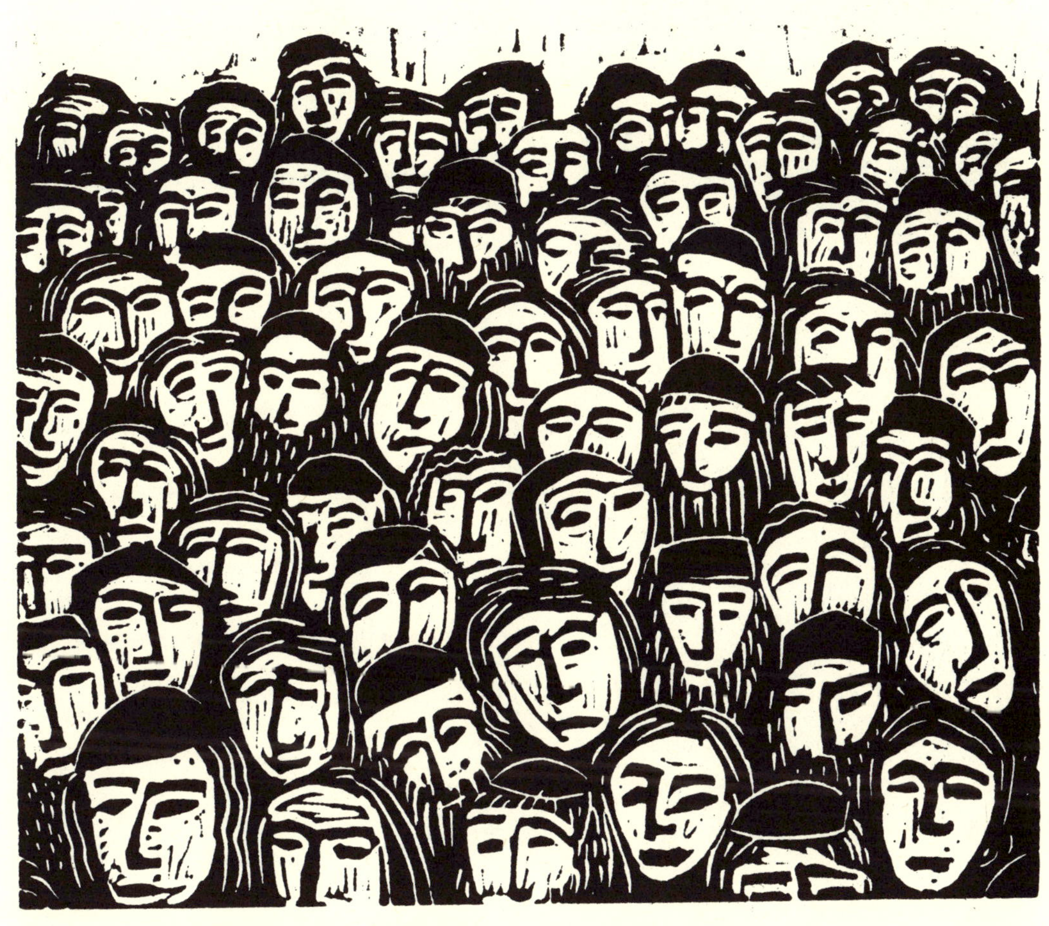

AT 5AM THE NAZIS TOOK US TO A SYNAGOGUE IN THE PROVINCIAL CAPITAL WITH THOUSANDS OF OTHER JEWS. SOON WE WERE MOVED TO A GHETTO, THEN THE TRAINS STARTED. WHEN OUR TURN CAME WE WERE LOCKED IN A CATTLE CAR SO CROWDED WE HAD TO SLEEP STANDING UP.

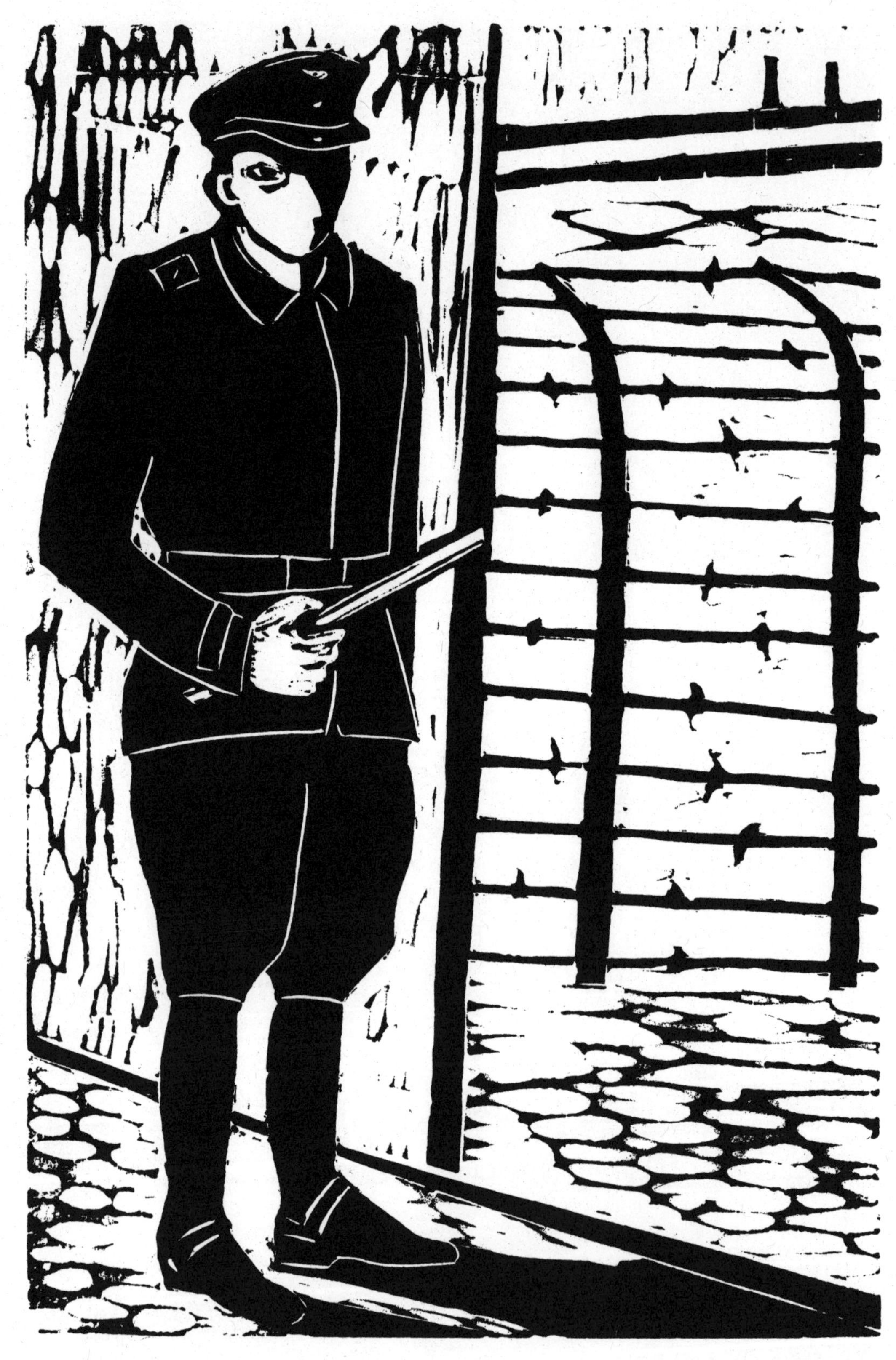

AFTER FOUR DAYS THE DOORS OPENED. SOLDIERS YELLED "RAUS! RAUS!" WE WERE IN AUSCHWITZ.

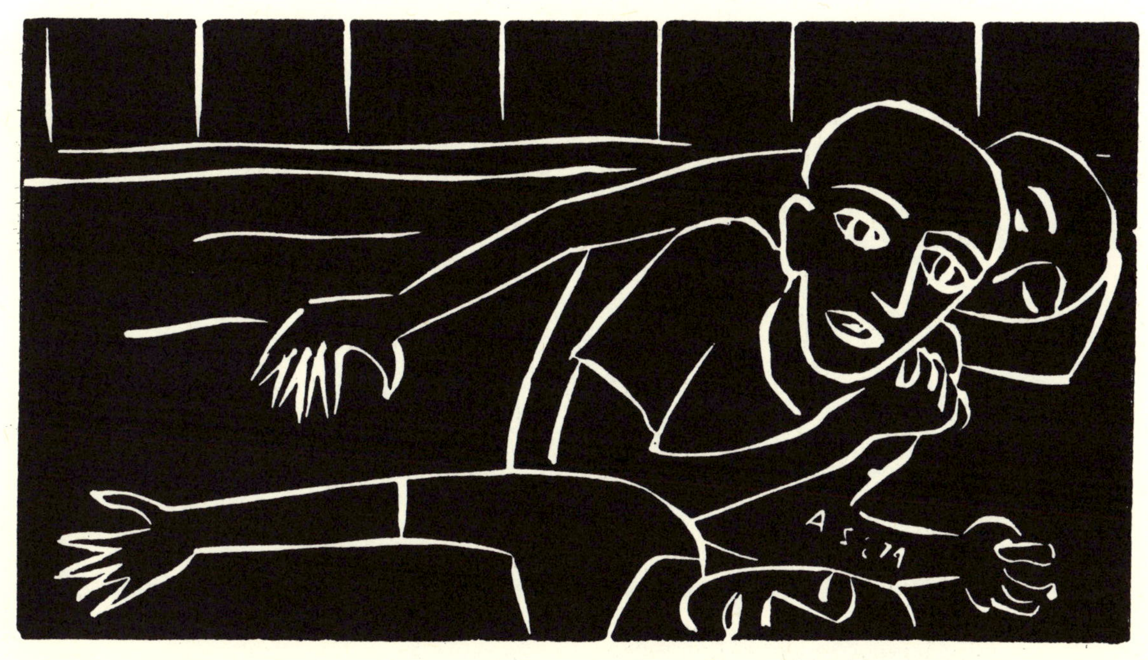

HEADS SHAVED, ARMS TATTOOED,
WE WERE SENT TO BARRACKS.
NEXT MORNING MY MOTHER, MY
SISTER AND I WERE SET TO WORK
SORTING AND PACKING CLOTHING,
SHOES, GLASSES FOR SHIPMENT
TO GERMANY. NIGHT AND DAY
THICK BLACK SMOKE FILLED THE
CAMP WITH AN AWFUL STENCH.
AFTER A FEW DAYS I COMPLETELY
LOST ALL MY SENSE OF SMELL.

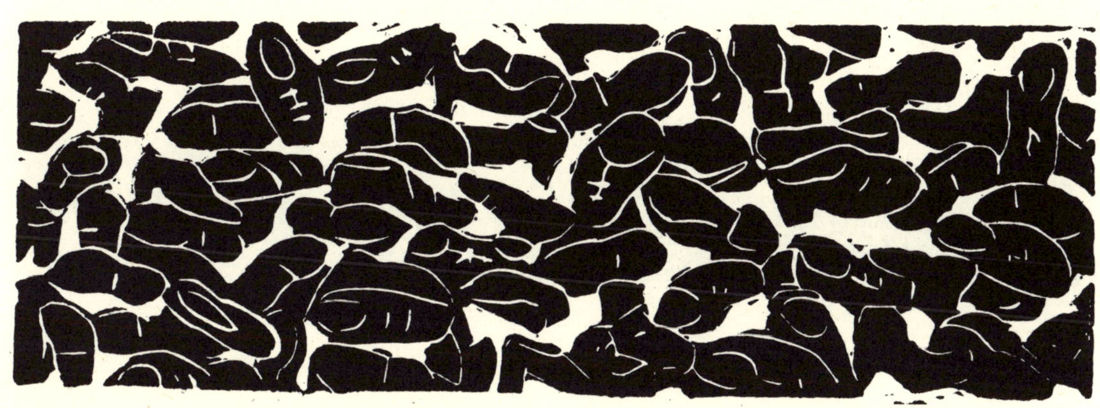

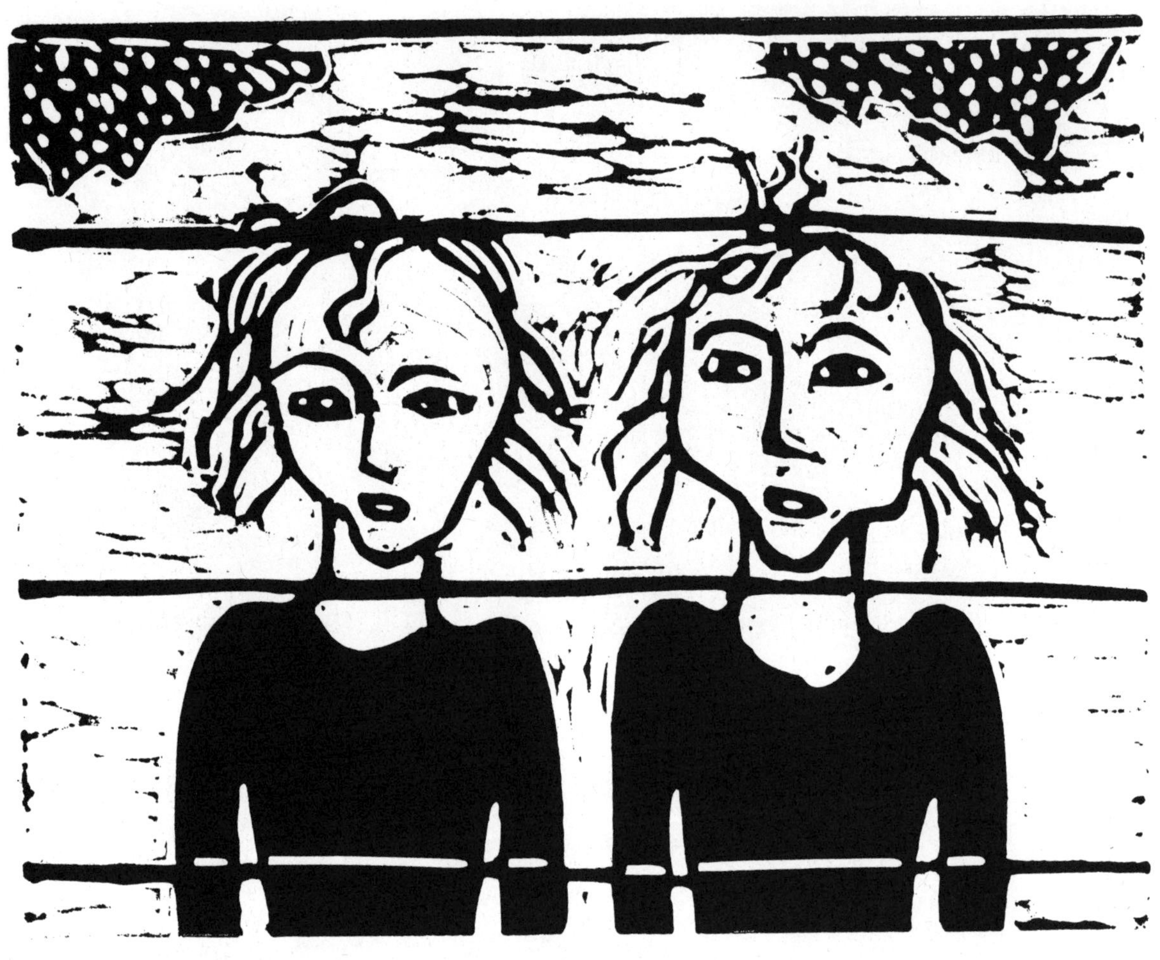

DR MENGELE CONDUCTED HIS EXPERIMENTS ON TWINS NEXT TO OUR WORKPLACE. WHEN WE FOUND FOOD MY MOTHER THREW SOME OVER THE FENCE TO THE TWINS. ALTHOUGH SHE WAS CAUGHT, SHE WAS NOT KILLED BECAUSE MY SISTER WAS THE BEST WORKER THEY HAD. ONCE SHE WAS REWARDED WITH FOOD FOR HER GOOD WORK.

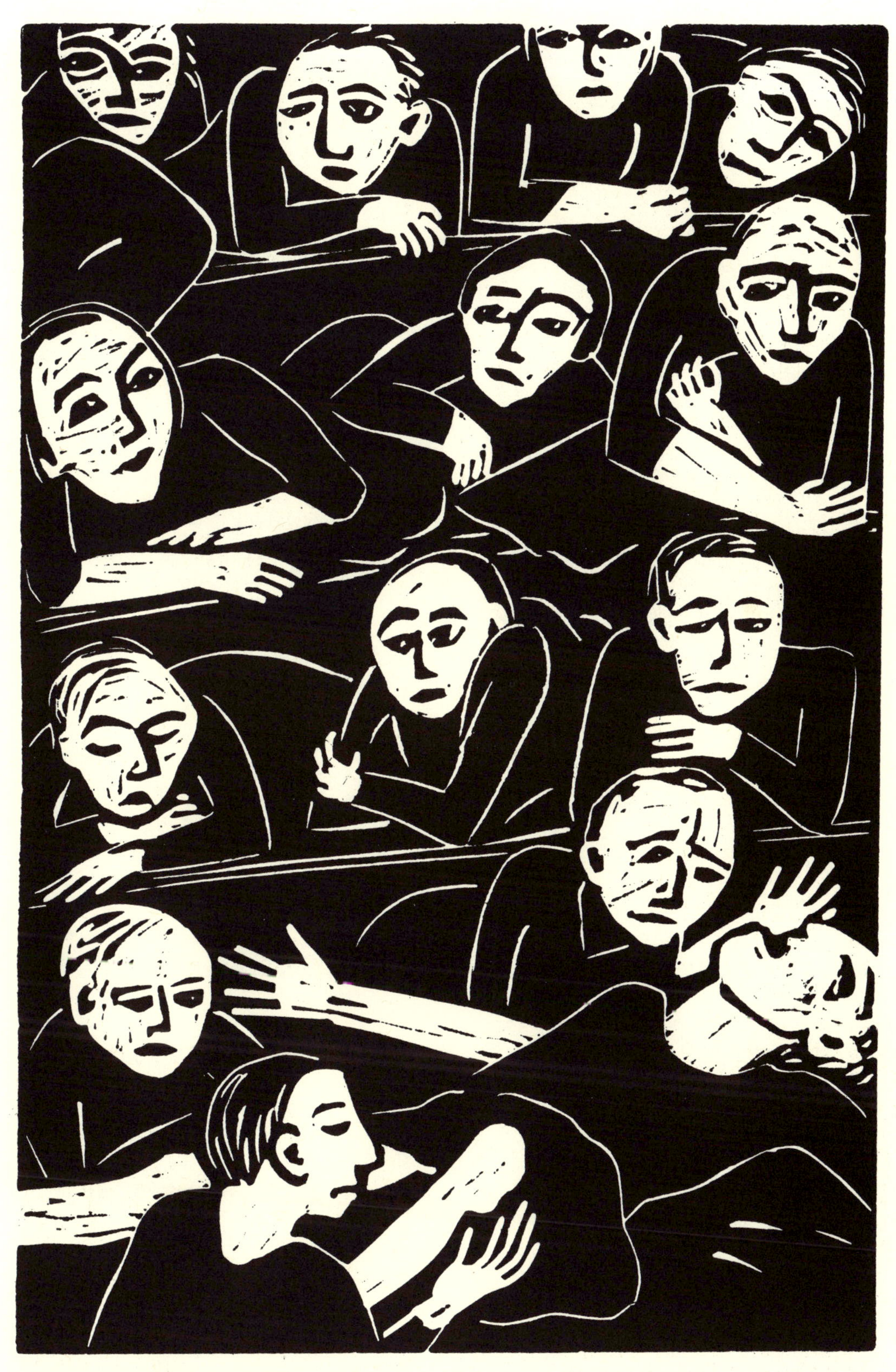

ONE NIGHT I WATCHED A SECRET OPERATION FROM MY BUNK. SEVERAL INMATES HELPED THE DOCTOR AND MUFFLED THE WOMAN'S SCREAMS.

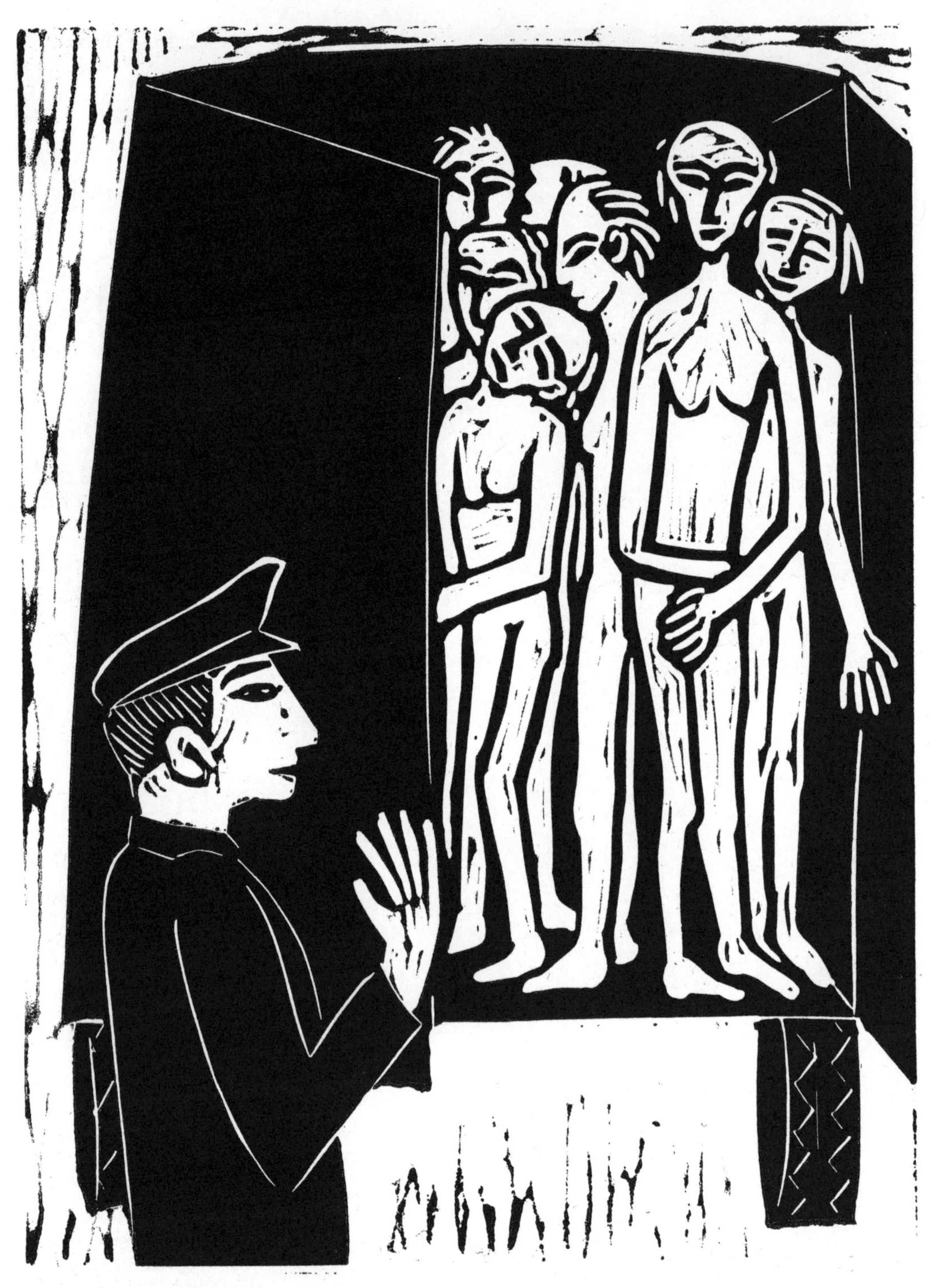

I GOT THINNER AND THINNER. LATE IN 1944 DR. MENGELE PICKED ME OUT IN A SELECTION. WITH THE OTHER SELECTED WOMEN I WAS LOADED IN A TRUCK, A HUNGARIAN GUARD WARNED ME WE WERE GOING TO THE GAS, HE TOLD ME HOW TO JUMP OFF AND ESCAPE

WHEN THE TRUCK STOPPED AT A GATE I ASKED THE OTHER WOMEN TO ESCAPE WITH ME. NO ONE WOULD. BUT I KNEW I WOULD BE KILLED IF I STAYED IN THE TRUCK, AND WOULD NEVER SEE MY MOTHER AGAIN. SO I TOOK A CHANCE AND JUMPED.

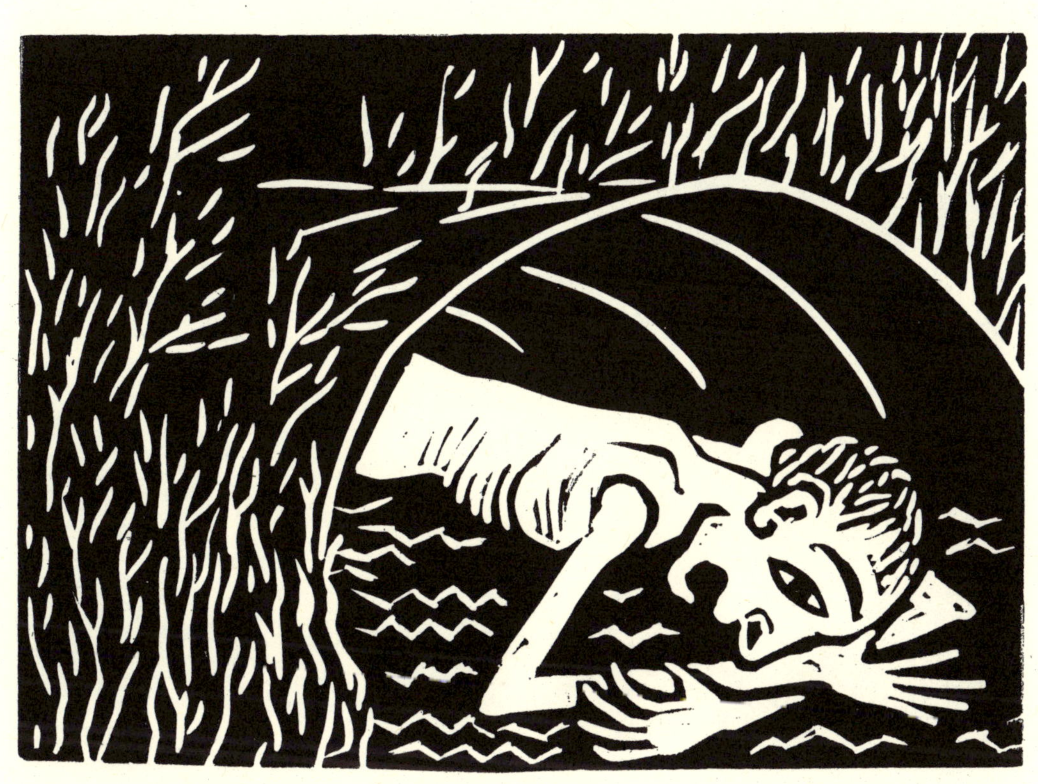

I FELL DOWN A BANK INTO A DITCH. I SAW A CULVERT AND I CRAWLED IN, HIDING NAKED IN THE ICY WATER. AT FIRST, I HEARD SIRENS AND GERMAN VOICES, AND THEN IT WAS QUIET. I DIDN'T MOVE UNTIL THE NEXT NIGHT. I FOLLOWED A LIGHT TO A BARRACKS. I CLIMBED INTO A BUNK, AND A WOMAN GAVE ME A COAT. IN THE MORNING WE WERE SENT TO ANOTHER CAMP.

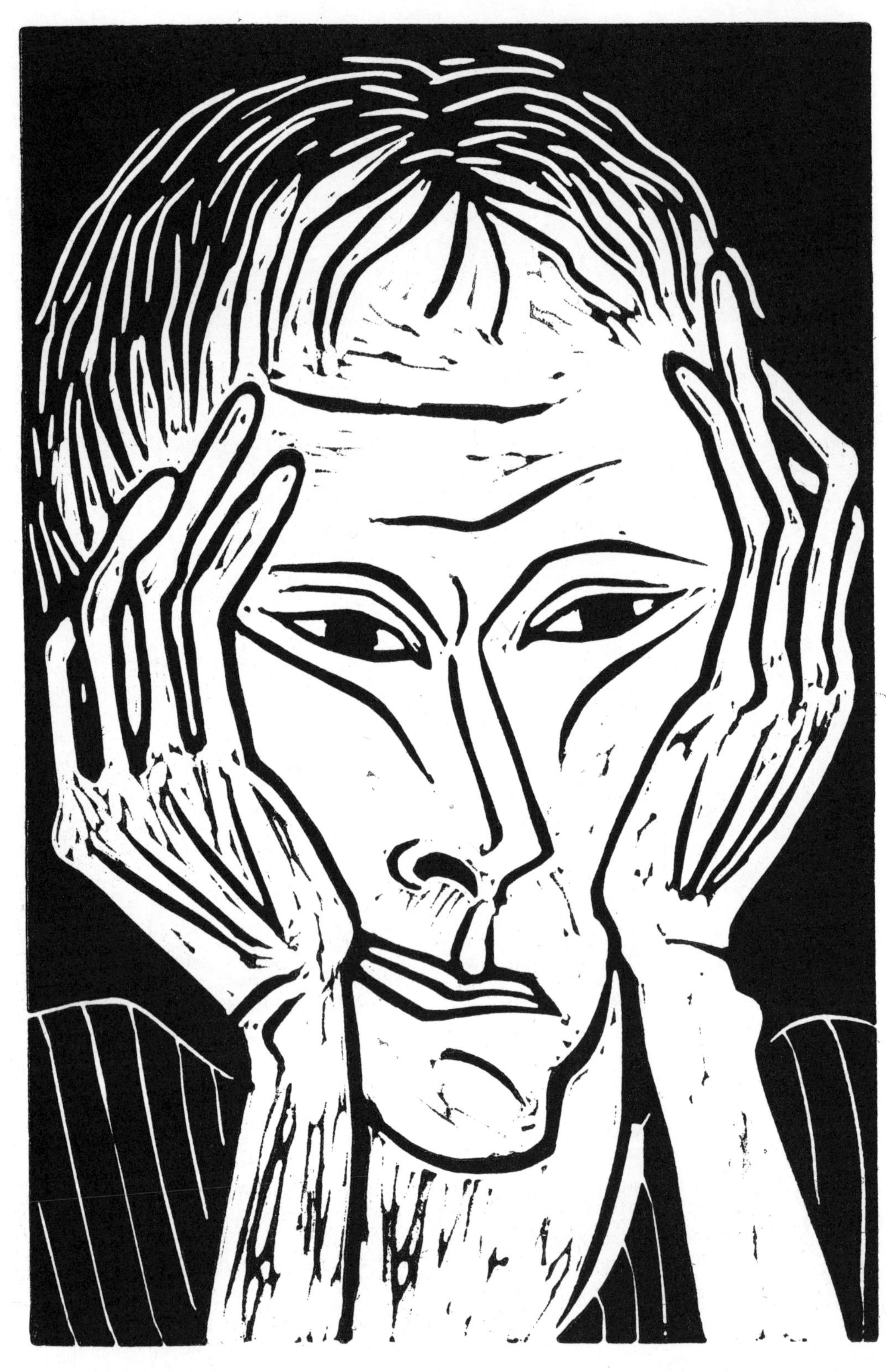

AS I WAS SENT FROM CAMP TO CAMP I WORRIED ABOUT AND MISSED MY MOTHER. AS THE WAR ENDED, I WAS PUT IN A TRAIN. WE HAD NO FOOD OR WATER. HALF THE WOMEN DIED.

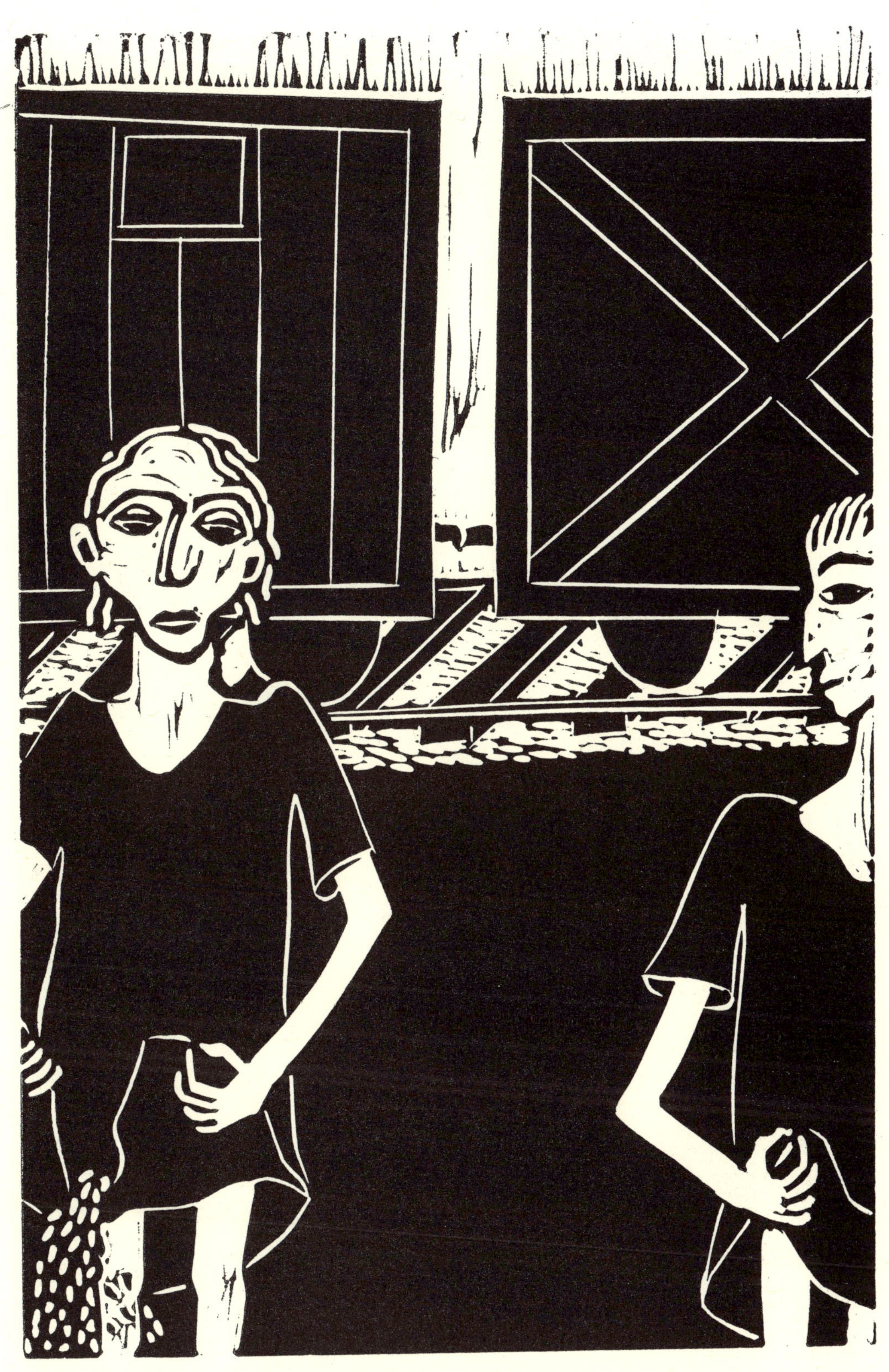

THE TRAIN STOPPED IN A FIELD. WE THREW OUT THE DEAD, THEN LINED UP FOR FOOD. MY DRESS WAS TORN AND MY FOOD FELL. I BENT OVER AND THE SS BEAT ME UNTIL I PASSED OUT.

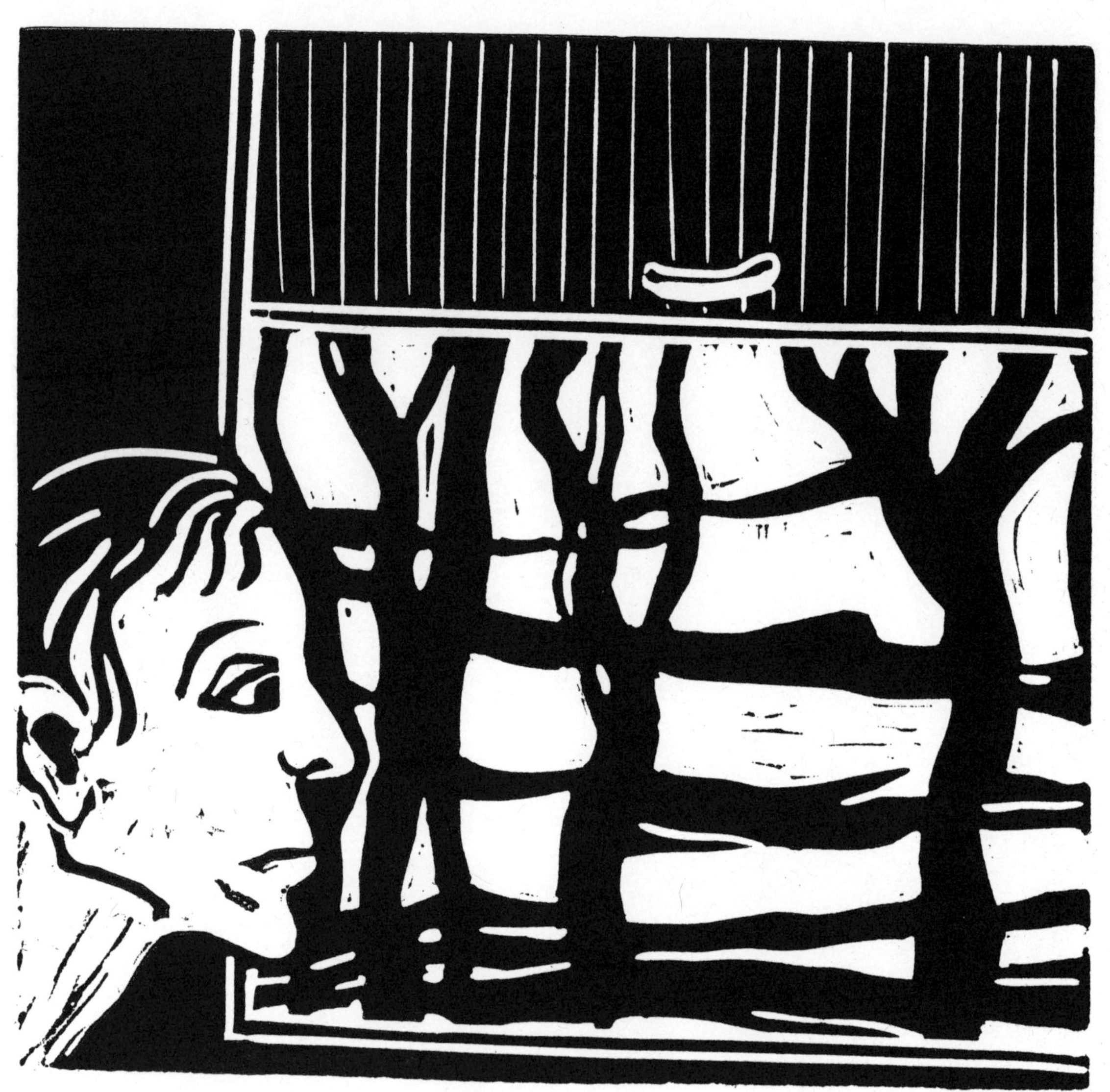

WHEN I AWOKE, I WAS IN A REAL PASSENGER TRAIN. WE HAD BEEN RESCUED BY THE SWEDISH RED CROSS. I WAS TAKEN IN BY A SWEDISH FAMILY. MOST OF MY FAMILY ALSO SURVIVED AND WENT HOME. WHEN I HAD A CHANCE TO GO TO THE USA MY MOTHER WROTE FROM THE USSR TELLING ME TO GO, EVEN THOUGH SHE MIGHT NEVER SEE ME AGAIN.

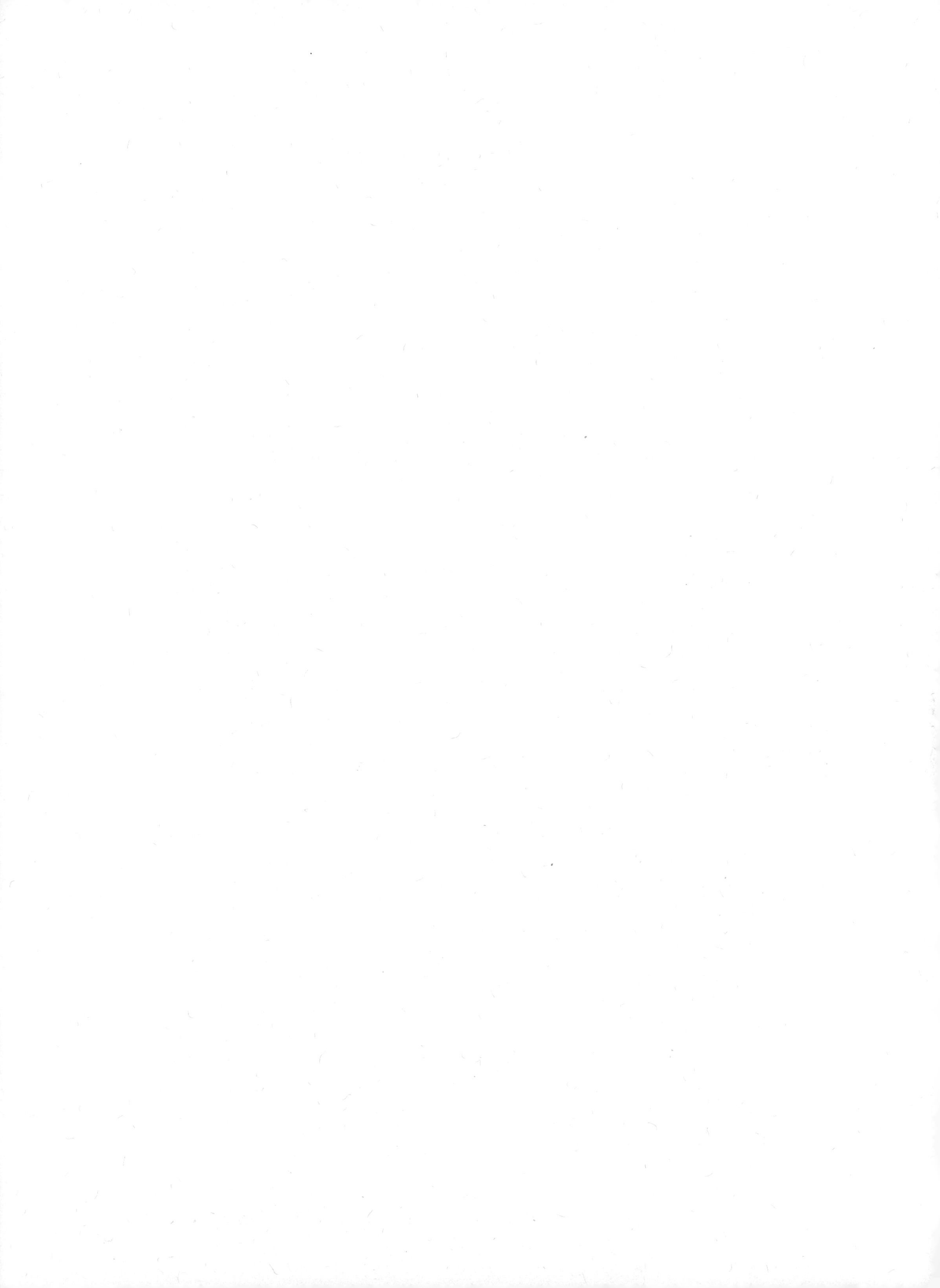

ABOUT THE AUTHOR

BARBARA MILMAN's paintings, prints, and mixed media works have been shown nationally since the early 1980s. She is a member of the California Society of Printmakers, the National Women's Caucus for Art, and the National Association of Women Artists. Since 1981, she has had over twenty-five solo shows and has participated in over one hundred group shows. Her artwork has won thirteen prizes, including a printmaking award from the National Association of Women Artists, has been published in art magazines, and is included in public and university collections.

Since 1990, much of Barbara Milman's work has focused on Jewish themes, particularly the Holocaust. In 1994, she led a panel entitled "Jewish Women's Artistic Identity" at the National Conference of the Women's Caucus for Art in New York City; and she was a member of a similar panel on Jewish women artists at the 1995 Jewish Women's Conference in San Francisco. In 1997, she participated in an exhibition of Miriam's Cups at New York's Hebrew Union College—Jewish Institute of Religion.

The original prints upon which this book is based were handprinted by the artist in a limited edition of twenty-five. A full set of the prints is included in the collection of the Zimmerli Museum at Rutgers University; additional prints are part of the Holocaust Collection at Vanderbilt University.

Barbara Milman received a J.D. from the Columbia University School of Law and spent twenty-five years practicing law, starting as a civil rights lawyer in Mississippi in 1996. Her last legal job was as chief counsel to the Assembly Rules Committee of the California State Legislature. She presently resides in Davis, California where she is a fulltime artist.